* This is a true story. Some names and other identifying information have been changed.

Cover and interior design by Dean Pickup

Front cover image: Dreamstime

Project management by Kingsley Publishing Services

www.kingsleypublishing.ca

First published in the United States in 2011 by Kingsley Publishing

Printed in Canada by Friesens
2011 / 2

Library and Archives Canada Cataloguing in Publication

Beach, Spencer, 1974-
In case of fire : please remain calm then slowly rebuild your life / Spencer Beach with Naomi K. Lewis.

ISBN 978-1-926832-01-2

1. Beach, Spencer, 1974-. 2. Fires--Casualties--Biography. 3. Burns and scalds--Patients--Biography. I. Lewis, Naomi K., 1976- II. Title.

RD96.4.B43 2010 617.1'1092 C2010-903120-2

To Trzok,

When life gets you down, get up and move on. You'll never experience the road ahead if you don't take the journey

Spencer Beach

This book is for Tina Beach, for standing by me and for making a hard life worth living. You are my best friend. May your pure and genuine heart always be filled with happiness and love. And for Amber and Aiden, whose little smiles fill the world with joy. May God be with you and bless all your days.

I love the Lord, for He heard my voice; He heard my cry for mercy.

Because He turned His ear to me, I will call on Him as long as I live.

- Psalm 116:1–2

Table of Contents

Whatever It Takes

"What's your name?"

"Spencer," I said. "Spencer Beach."

"How old are you, Spencer?"

"Twenty nine."

"When were you born?"

"February 20, 1974."

"Okay, you're doing fine."

"My life is over. I'm dead. I'm going to die."

"My name's Randy. I'm a paramedic. We're on our way to the hospital. Do you remember what happened?"

"I was in a fire. My life is over. I don't want to die!"

"Where do you live, Spencer?"

"Don't let my wife see me!"

"What's your wife's name?"

I tried to look out the back of the ambulance. The sunlight hurt my eyes. The acrid smell of burnt flesh overwhelmed my senses. My groin and lips were swelling, and hurt like they'd been stung by a thousand bees.

"Talk to me," the paramedic said. "What's your wife's name?"

"Tina. It's Tina. Promise you won't let her see me!"

"Where is Tina today?"

"That lady back there called her cellphone. But you can't let her see me. Promise me. Why am I still alive? Where's the hospital?"

"It'll be less than five minutes now. Hold on, buddy."

"What happened to my lips? My lips hurt! Are my fingers still there? Are my ears still there? My penis?"

The clothes I had been wearing were mostly burned away, and what was left had melted onto my body.

"They're all there."

"My wife's pregnant. Four months. She can't see me like this."

"Two minutes now, Spencer."

"Will I die soon? I'm dead!"

"One minute."

"My wife's pregnant. Oh, God. My wife's pregnant. God, please let me die before she sees me like this."

"Thirty seconds."

I felt the ambulance drop steeply downhill and saw the scorching light of the sun disappear. I thought I was descending headfirst into a basement.

Everything was hazy and strange. The paramedic who'd talked me through the ride was gone, and a crowd of strangers lifted a white sheet so it filled my field of vision like a tent, then settled over me, head to toe. It was a shroud. *I must be dead,* I thought, as I felt the gurney rolling. Part of my mind clicked into reality, and I realized they'd covered me with a sheet because my injuries were so severe. They didn't want anyone to see me as they wheeled me through the hospital.

When the sheet was pulled back from my face, I saw that I was in a private room. A group of nurses lifted me off the gurney and lay me on the floor, where I shivered with cold. I tried to blink against the glaring fluorescent light. I forced myself to think. *What was I doing on the floor, huddled in a corner?* My mind kept slipping between panicked confusion and clear, rational thought. I realized I was still on the gurney. People hovered around me, lifting the sheet, examining me. I was too afraid to look at my body, so I turned my head sideways. I couldn't seem to close my eyes.

"Spencer."

A tall, grey-haired man was beside me. He spoke in a steady voice, and his presence was comforting.

"I'm Dr. Prichard," he said. "I'm head of the University of Alberta burn unit. I want you to know we have the best burn unit in Canada."

"Burn unit?"

"Spencer, can you tell me how you were burned?"

"A fire," I said. "I was in a fire."

"What were you doing when the fire started?"

"Stripping lino."

"How were you stripping the lino?"

"With a contact thinner."

"A chemical fire?"

Another voice confirmed that this was the case.

"How bad is it?" I asked. "I need to know."

Dr. Prichard lifted the sheet that covered me and looked me up and down.

"You have third and fourth degree burns over 90 percent of your body," he said. He took a couple of seconds to think about it and then said, "You have a 5 percent chance to live. Spencer, I have to ask you this question while you're conscious and lucid. We have two options here. You can fight to live, and I'll do everything I can for you, or I can make sure you're comfortable and let you go. It's up to you. If you choose to fight, it will be a long road. We'll do the best we can, and we have an excellent facility here, but I can't promise anything." His voice became a blur. I heard phrases like "compassionate care," "quality of life," "skin grafts," and "permanent disabilities and disfigurement."

"Do you understand?" Dr. Prichard asked.

Of course, on a fundamental level, I didn't and couldn't understand. An hour earlier, I'd had a 100 percent chance to live. I was finishing up a flooring job so I could head home to see my wife. I was going to spend the evening planning my buddy's stag.

In the ambulance, I had begged for death. But now the panic was gone, and I was strangely calm. There was no question in my mind. Through the fog, three of Dr. Prichard's words stood out: "chance to live."

"I don't care," I said. "Do what it takes. I don't want to die."

• • •

For most of my twenty-ninth year, I lay in a hospital bed, immobile and unable to speak, eat, or breathe on my own. I lay there through my wife's pregnancy and the birth of our child, in a haze of painkillers and anti-depressants, anger eating away at my soul as I gradually had parts of my fingers and face amputated, and 90 percent of the skin on my body replaced. I replayed, again and again, the fire that had put me there. The fire my doctors assumed I couldn't remember. *It's a mistake*, I thought, sometimes. *It's a nightmare*. But I could still hear and smell the fire all around me. Sometimes I still can.

I lay there for seven months before I looked in a mirror. When the big day came, my wife and a hospital psychologist sat on either side of my bed. Since I couldn't move my arms or sit up, Tina had to hold the mirror for me. I was more afraid of that object in her hands than I had been of all the surgical tools and machines and pills I'd faced.

"I'm ready," I said.

Tina held the mirror over my face.

She had warned me, as this day approached; she'd done her best to prepare me for what I'd see. She told me I'd lost most of my nose and ears, and that my eyelids and lips had been reconstructed imperfectly. She told me my hair was gone. She'd warned me about the skin grafts that hadn't yet healed, and about the scars that were already forming.

But nothing could have prepared me for what I saw. I had no idea who that guy was. I looked at a big scab on what was left of the bridge of my nose. I stared up at that precise point for three minutes. Somehow, I didn't take in anything else. There was too much. I was looking at the face of a stranger. How could I have changed so much, in an accident that lasted less than thirty seconds?

"Please take it away." I had seen enough.

Before Tina left that day, I asked to look in the mirror once more, and she held it up for me. Again, I just stared, unable to grasp the details, unable to absorb how much had changed. I tried to find something familiar in that reflection. There was nothing. I knew my eyes, at least, would be the same, and I avoided them. To look myself in the eyes would mean admitting that guy was me.

• • •

One day, over five years later, in the fall of 2008, I walked through security in the Edmonton, Alberta, airport, on my way to catch a plane.

The man behind the security belt looked at my boarding pass, never looking directly at my face, except for that unintentional, awkward glance I always seem to get. He asked me where I was going.

"Just to Calgary."

"For business?"

"Yes. I'm shooting a video."

"Oh, yeah?"

"I'm a movie star," I joked. In fact, I was meeting a group of executives from Texas, who were flying in to tape one of my presentations and interview me for a safety video.

The other security official, a small, pretty, middle-aged woman, was eyeing me from the other side of the x-ray machine. I was so used to people staring at me, I barely noticed. The pretty security official couldn't take her eyes off me. I knew it was either because I looked familiar from my TV appearances, or because I'd been working out. Or most likely because she couldn't help but wonder what had happened to me.

"Excuse me," she said at last, as I reached for my bags and grabbed one strap with the fused fingers of my left hand. "I know this may be a strange question, but are you a professional speaker?"

"It's not a strange question. Yes, I am."

"Were you in Fort McMurray last week?"

"Yes, that was me."

"My son saw you speak," she said. "He works up in the oil sands. This is so strange that you're here. I mean, he told me your whole story. You had such an impact on him."

"Well, thank you. That's great to hear."

"What's your name? Something Beach ..."

"Spencer Beach."

"Spencer Beach," she said. She shook her head. "Just amazing. What a story, sir. I have to congratulate you." She watched me put on my jacket, taking note of how I managed the zipper with my partial fingers. "You seem like such a happy person," she said. "How do you do it?"

By then, it was strange to me that people expected me to be unhappy. I knew I looked odd from the outside, but from my perspective, the world looked perfect. Five years earlier, I was given a 5 percent chance to live. I went from doctors telling me I might never walk again to being able to run and ski with my daughter. I was told I would never work again, but I went to university and became a construction safety officer. I dedicated my life to counselling injured workers, speaking to children about fire prevention, helping peers overcome depression, and, most of all, striving to change the culture that leads so many workers to devastating or fatal accidents.

"What's not to be happy about?" I told that security officer. "I'm living my life."

I am a professional speaker, a father, and a joyous, grateful man. And all this happened thanks to a series of realizations I can sum up in three simple truths. First, God never abandoned me. Second, my family and friends never gave up on me. And third, I counteracted the poison left after my accident by realizing the source of the poisoning: myself.

• • •

Beach Brothers

Six years after the fire, I still dream again and again that I look down at my arms and, to my surprise, find the skin smooth and tanned. I run my fingertips over my wrists to feel the tickle of soft, light hairs. In the mirror, I see a strong, healthy man with thick blond hair, and when I grin at myself, dimples crease my cheeks. I turn to see the contours of my nose and ears. I think, *What was I so upset about? The burns aren't that bad at all.* Relief floods over me; the weight of the fire lifts away. That feeling lasts for a few seconds after I open my eyes. And then I remember.

No matter how many times I examine myself, no matter how many strangers pass me on the street and turn their heads, pretending to check a store window, no matter how many times I struggle to accomplish daily tasks with my partly amputated fingers, I still look like my old self in my dreams. I still have my fingers and my hair, and my nose and my ears. I have smooth, evenly coloured skin. I have nipples. I sweat to keep cool in the summer, and my circulation keeps me warm in the winter. I'm the kind of guy girls look at on the street, but not because of burn scars.

I don't see myself the way others see me; *I* am not burnt. When people stare at me or handle me with kid gloves, I know why they're doing it, but I don't expect or want it. I expect to be treated the same way I was treated before. Like Two-Face, the Batman villain who changes after half his face is disfigured in a fire, I am two people, in my case existing one inside the other. On the outside, I have the face everyone else sees—the face of a burn survivor. But inside, I have the face I see—the face of a normal guy. The same normal guy I was for twenty-nine years.

• • •

My life began comfortably and without drama in St. Albert, a suburb of Edmonton, Alberta. Back in the seventies, St. Albert was more like a small town. Our three-bedroom bungalow was custom designed by an architect friend of my father's, but I doubt that architect chose the hideous gold shag carpet that lay throughout the main level. We had an atrium and an unfinished basement until my father decided to turn both into bedrooms so my two brothers and I wouldn't kill each other.

My oldest brother, Reagan, was born in 1971, on New Year's Eve, and Craig was born two years later, in February. I was born last, in 1974, and as I grew into a toddler, I looked nothing like either of my parents or my brothers. Both my brothers take after my father: they are dark haired with serious faces, and their eyes are wide set, suggesting intelligence and complexity. I was blond and blue eyed, and my dimples matched a mischievous, light-hearted disposition. I was so excitable as a child, I once leapt out of my chair at the end of the school day, grabbed my bag, ran down the hallway and out the door. My mother, waiting for me outside, watched me sprint down the stairs and smash right into a metal bar. I almost broke my nose.

Reagan and Craig used to tell me I looked different because I was the mailman's son. And that was the least of their teasing. According to Craig, Reagan harassed him until I came along, and then they both turned on me. By harassed, I mean tormented, tortured, and abused. If you think I'm exaggerating, picture a tiny blond boy forced to stand on the edge of an old tub in the garage, tied by his wrists to the roof, and hit repeatedly with a paddle. Luckily, that time, a friend of mine came by and freed me, and we got our revenge by tying Reagan to a tree. I won't tell you what we did to him before walking away.

Craig had more subtle methods. When it was his night to do the dishes, he washed about half the plates and utensils, and hid the rest in cupboards or under the sink. The next night, when it was my turn, my pile always seemed strangely large. It took me ages to catch on to why Craig was always helping me out by delivering more dirty dishes that I "forgot."

Reagan's attacks slowed down after one of them ended in disaster. He was already in high school when he and his friend ambushed me one day after school and chased me through the house with a fishing rod they had broken in two. I ran into my room and slammed my door on the fibreglass rod. I grabbed the half inside my room, opened my door, and whipped the rod at my brother. The splintered end hit him in the eye.

There was a lot of blood. Reagan's friend leaned over him in horror.

"Dude, your eye's gone!"

"But I can see," Reagan said. "I can see sparkles."

His eye was still there and functioning, but it was full of fibreglass shards that had to be picked out in Emergency. Reagan had to wear bandages over his eye for a month, while he healed. Then, for years, shards occasionally worked their way out of his eye, each requiring a gruesome visit to the specialist for "drill flushing." It was only in 2008 that he was finally allowed to wear contact lenses.

My constant battles with my brothers taught me resilience; I could suffer nasty surprises and pain on a daily basis, and none of it really got to me. Reagan and Craig weren't sure it was a compliment when I said their childhood torment helped prepare me for my recovery after the fire.

"C'mon, man," said Reagan. "You're one of my best friends."

And that's true. But I wasn't always.

My mother worried a bit more about my battles with my brothers than my father did.

"I'm just grateful they're healthy and full of energy," my dad used to say.

"Sure ..." My mother was not entirely convinced that Craig and Reagan's daily attacks would make me stronger. Her faith in my dad's parenting techniques was still recovering from the time she came home to find one-year-old Craig bouncing in his Jolly Jumper, sucking uneasily on a soother attached to his head with several rounds of Scotch tape.

"He kept spitting it out," Dad said, from the couch, where he was absorbed in a hockey game.

But even when I was little, life with my brothers wasn't all about padding my clothes with cushions for their daily attacks. We had fun, too. Our house was on an oddly shaped crescent with north- and east-facing exits, and the best part was the park across the street; it had two outdoor skating rinks—one public and one for hockey. In the winter, we skated almost every day. Behind the house was a ravine, so during the summers my brothers and I did a lot of adventuring. Just on the other side of the park were farmers' fields, and in those fields was bush, where we spent our days building forts. As of 2010, my parents still live in that house, though of course it's a good fifteen-minute walk to any fields, now.

• • •

One of the things I've always admired about my parents is that they've never fought for long, and have always treated each other with respect. I started praying for true love as soon as I could form the thought—even as a child, I was looking forward to marriage. As far as I was concerned, it was never too early to find my soulmate; my parents, after all, met when they were five years old—or eleven, depending on which of them you ask.

My mother, Andrea, is smart and composed, has the strong memory Reagan and I inherited, and loves to read. She's not afraid to do whatever it takes to make her family comfortable. Though she will talk in depth when she's at ease, she doesn't engage in conversation with just anyone. My dad, Don, is the opposite in that respect. His greatest joy is socializing, and he's the life of every party. He loves to tell stories and jokes, and he makes friends at the drop of a hat. Often, before my dad even knows what he's thinking, he's saying it. I inherited that from him.

My mother was born in Latvia; my great-grandfather had been a duke, but the Second World War wiped out the family's wealth. My grandparents, great uncle, and uncle went to Germany and ended up living in camps. That's where my mother was born. In 1949, they had the choice to go to Austria, the U.S., or Canada. They chose Canada. It wasn't long before my grandfather abandoned the family, leaving my grandmother alone with two children in a log cabin in Saskatchewan. They never saw him again.

I guess resilience runs in my family, because my grandmother moved from place to place, working as a housekeeper to support herself and her children. Eventually, she married the man I knew as Grandpa Jekabson, and they moved to a five-acre farm in Winterburn, Alberta, near Edmonton. One day, my mother and her brother saw a lone little boy playing on their neighbour's lawn, so they went over to keep him company. It turned out the neighbour's pastor was visiting, and that boy was his grandson. It was on that lawn, my father says, that he first met my mother, when they were both five. My mother has no memory of the incident.

If not for a first devastating fire, my parents would likely have never married, and I wouldn't exist: when Mom was nine, her family's farm burned down. Left homeless, they moved into Edmonton and it was there that they started attending church regularly—the same church their old neighbours attended. That's where my mother remembers meeting my father, whose grandfather was still the church's pastor. My parents were both eleven, and classmates in Sunday school. The pastor had three sons, and my dad's father, William Beach, was the second. Grandpa Beach, as I knew him, had founded Edmonton's first flooring company in 1937 with his brothers, and they called it Beach Brothers. My grandfather was a linoleum expert who won awards for the designs he created in hotels, and my father was learning the trade.

My parents were confirmed in that same church, and they joined the young people's club. All throughout their high school years, my father used to pick up my mother on his motorbike and take her to those meetings, and he often visited her family just to play cards. He jokes he was over at her house every second night, so he figured he might as well marry her. They started dating when they were eighteen, and when they were twenty, my dad took my mother to the A&W drive-through and told her he intended to marry her.

"You don't tell me that," she said. "You ask."

So he climbed out of the car, got down on one knee, and proposed properly.

"I don't know why she chose me," Dad still says.

It's fitting that my parents got to know each other at church, because their faith was so important to both of them, and one of the most important things they'd teach my brothers and me. Their families were conservative evangelical Lutherans, and as children both my parents found comfort and wisdom in the scriptures. My mother grew up with a grandmother who taught her about God and Jesus, and how He sustains us, and that stayed with her all her life. Of course, my father's grandfather, being a pastor, often talked to his grandchildren about Bible passages and stories.

My parents strived to pass on the wisdom their grandparents and parents had given them. We all went to St. Peter's Lutheran Church every Sunday. We always prayed before meals, and I remember my mother leading Craig and me in the Lord's Prayer every night as we lay in our bunk beds, before she said a special prayer for us. Then one night she said we were ready to say our own prayers, like Reagan did. Everything my parents taught me about spirituality always rang true. As evangelical Lutherans, we hold at the heart of our faith the word of God: we follow the Bible without adding to it or taking anything away. My parents always told me what the Bible says: that, as humans, we all must suffer, but that God never gives us more than we can bear. They assured me my fate was in benevolent hands. After the fire, those insights, so ingrained throughout my childhood, would save me from a depression that could easily have destroyed my life.

• • •

My parents both worked to pay the mortgage, so when we were little, my brothers and I had a full-time babysitter. When that babysitter moved away, we went into daycare. One afternoon, our caregiver phoned Mom and told her that Craig was at the hospital, getting stitches in his chin. It turned out the caregiver had pushed Craig into the garbage can. My mother, not willing to trust another stranger with us, quit her job immediately.

That was the end of daycare for us. But my mother still needed an income. So she started babysitting two neighbouring brothers every day, and they became our best friends. During those years, my mother took care of five boys all day and then waitressed in the evening after my father came home. As I said, she's always been willing to do whatever it took to make her family comfortable, and I looked forward to having my own family so I could do the same for them.

I was so eager to plan for a prosperous adult life, I happily started going on jobs with my father when I was eight, carrying tools and materials and helping with the cleanup. The first job I remember was in a church. Craig and I carried about thirty sheets of plywood, which was a heavy load for us. It was fun to spend that time with my father, and I enjoyed feeling useful. It seemed natural that I was already learning the trade so I could someday continue the legacy my grandfather and his brothers began. The work was challenging and interesting, and occasionally action packed.

When I was eleven or twelve, my dad had a job renovating the washrooms for a pizza restaurant in an Edmonton strip mall. "I need your help tonight," he told Craig and me over dinner. Reagan was older and had his own part-time work. Dad said, "We need to get the ceramic off those walls after the place closes."

We left the house as the sun set, and drove into Edmonton. Dad led me and Craig through the pizza joint's kitchen, gave us each a hammer, and the three of us started smashing.

Craig took a break to carry a load of debris out to the dumpster, but he barely made it through the back door when he heard, "Freeze!" Craig stopped in disbelief—he was surrounded by armed police officers, their guns aimed right at him. Apparently, the clerk in the convenience store next door had heard our banging and thought we were breaking down the wall to rob him. Those cops must have been as surprised as my brother when they realized they had a thirteen-year-old boy in their sights, boxes of broken tiles in hand. Craig managed to explain the situation, and the officers came inside to see my father and me still hard at work.

I grew up thinking highly of my parents and grandparents, watching all of them create their own livelihoods through trial and error and innovation. My mother started several businesses, including importing ginger from Hawaii, before she starting managing farmers' markets, where she also sells pickled vegetables. She runs her farmers' market business to this day. My Grandpa Jekabson was the smartest adult I knew; he was an engineer, owned a concrete block company, and had developed a new lightweight, fire-resistant, soundproof concrete block. He was the one who taught my brothers and me to respect fire, but never to fear it. He showed us how to build a fire, and we used to make little cardboard army bases to place strategically around the wood so we could watch them burn.

During the summers, my mother used to pick up my grandmother and drive us all from St. Albert east through Edmonton and then outside the city limits to my Grandpa Jekabson's plant; it sat on so many acres, he'd set aside a portion of land for my mother and grandmother's garden. This was no ordinary garden, and I haven't seen anything like it since. It was enormous, and Mom and Grandma grew every vegetable I knew of—carrots, potatoes, onions, peas, and cabbage—you name it. Reagan, Craig, and I helped my mother and grandmother pull weeds, pick cabbages and beans, or tug carrots out of the ground until we got bored, or my grandmother became frustrated with one of us. She was always one to speak her mind—something I have in common with her—and that often led to a trail of shocked faces and hurt feelings. Luckily for me, I was always my grandmother's favourite and experienced the wealth of generosity often hidden beneath her no-holds-barred conversation style. To this day, I'd do anything for her. We spent the rest of those summer days in the plant, where we jumped in huge piles of sawdust, and sometimes my grandfather paid us to shoot pigeons. Since Grandpa Jekabson died when I was fourteen, I remember him mostly from those days in the plant. He always gave us cookies from his desk drawer, and once a day, he took us downstairs and bought us a pop. Since we were the boss's grandkids, everyone treated us well.

My other grandmother died before I was born, so I never knew her, but my paternal grandfather, Grandpa Beach, was the most physically fit person, for his age, I've ever known. He rode his bike to work even into his old age, and he worked with wood out in his shed until he was diagnosed with cancer. His greatest joy was sitting out on the ice or in a boat, fishing. He just found great pleasure in the ritual of it; he didn't do it for the fish, which he never ate. Instead, he brought his catch to a Japanese restaurant downtown. He was friends with the owner, who brought home my grandfather's fish and cooked it up for his family; in return, he prepared Grandpa a meal of chicken or fish with rice in his restaurant. Grandpa Beach became a true friend and mentor for me when I worked with him at Beach Brothers. We even went on jobs together so he could teach me new techniques.

• • •

But before I started working, I had to get through my teen years. By the time I began high school, the war with my brothers was pretty much over. The three of us were friends, and they'd already paved my way to popularity. Reagan had graduated from grade twelve and played guitar in a heavy metal band, and Craig, in grade eleven, was known for his easy-going, up-for-anything personality. And it didn't hurt that we were allowed to have parties. There was a party every weekend, and when it was at our house, everyone came. I loved holding court and leading the fun.

I enjoyed my neighbourhood as a child, and I enjoyed it as a teenager, but as an adult, I look back and wish I'd been more critical. There was too much money there, too much privilege, and because of that, a lot of drugs. My parents weren't rich, but a lot of the families around us were. Every day, the parents in my neighbourhood gave the kids money, and the kids took that cash to school, pooled it, and bought drugs. Of course, the drugs didn't attract everyone, but, unfortunately, they did attract me. One thing I've observed in my study of safety, injuries, and reckless behaviour in general is that people will go to amazing and often self-destructive lengths to fulfill their desires. My greatest desire, in my youth, was to be liked. In junior high school, I discovered that the drug users and drinkers accepted me, even looked up to me, and loved my outgoing, daredevil personality. I was separated from that group when we went to different high schools, but it didn't take me long to find the drug users in my new school, too. There were about forty people in my high school drug group, and though we were all friends with people outside that group, too, we gravitated together—for all the wrong reasons.

I was a good athlete, and excelled at high jump and hurdles. I was so confident—some might say cocky—about long distance running that I once stopped during a race to share a smoke with a buddy, and I still came in third. Looking back, I can see that smoke break resulted from my worst flaws. I felt invincible, and thought I didn't need to follow, or even know, the rules. That macho attitude attracted some people and made others think I was an asshole, a fact I didn't notice or care about at the time. My attitude also led me into a series of needless risks, and culminated when I was twenty-nine, in the accident that almost ended my life.

I also made the mistake of believing I could include drug use in a healthy lifestyle without it taking over. I was heavily into pot and drinking, and I'd taken up smoking. I tried acid and mushrooms a few times, too, but didn't like their mind-altering, hallucinatory effects. My drug of choice was cocaine, but I couldn't afford it very often. I was on a pot budget. Partying soon became the point of my life. Lethargic from being stoned all the time, I suffered a few hard knocks (literally—I kept missing the mat during high jump and landing on the floor) and finally gave up sports altogether.

Even then, I was a strategist. I developed a system that accommodated my lifestyle and allowed me to pass my classes: at the beginning of each semester, I studied as hard as I could and got my marks up as high as possible. After a couple of months, I had high enough averages in all my subjects that I could just drift. I partied for the rest of the semester, knowing I was guaranteed a 60 or 65 percent in each course. I did well enough that my parents never worried about me or thought I'd lost control of my life. Unfortunately, I felt like they were indifferent to my behaviour, and that feeling made me try even harder to get their—and everyone else's—attention.

It's incredible to think what grades I could have achieved if I'd continued studying throughout the year, but I was convinced the door to higher education was closed to me for financial reasons: I wasn't eligible for a loan, and my grades weren't high enough for a scholarship. I already knew I would be a floor layer. I'd known that since I was eight years old. I'm not saying I blame my parents or anyone else for my poor work ethic. I chose a lifestyle that sapped my ambition. All I wanted was to have fun, and my only concrete goals were to finish high school and then make a lot of money.

Of course, I rarely went to church as I entered my teens, and soon stopped going completely, except during the holidays and when my parents dragged me. I didn't want to think about how my behaviour might contradict the beliefs I still held dear, deep down inside. I didn't want to hear about responsibility or about life's meaning, and I was miles from realizing the preciousness of my time in this world. Back then, I didn't want to think too hard about anything at all.

• • •

Life of the Party

Throughout my teen years, besides having a good time, there was one other thing I wanted.

In junior high, I started praying each night for a girlfriend, one I could love. Even at that age, I wanted to find my companion and soulmate. And I wanted her to be beautiful, smart, thoughtful, and decent. My demands were high, but, although I went to school with girls and had some female friends, my understanding of dating and romance was non-existent.

When I started high school, I'd already had a couple of experiences that told me I was ready for love. In the summer after grade seven, I was camping in Kananaskis, in the Rocky Mountains, with my parents, when a girl left a note outside my tent. She'd written, "You're cute," and left directions to a meeting place. I was so nervous, I got lost trying to follow her directions, and by the time I found the place deep in the bush along a hiking trail, she was gone. I remember standing there in the trees, looking in awe at the mountains rising above me and the Kananaskis River running beside me, and feeling even more awe at the revelation that a real life girl had noticed me and pursued me.

For the rest of grades seven and eight, I noticed how easy it was to make girls giggle, and how they sometimes blushed and looked away when I smiled at them. By the summer before high school started, when I was fourteen, I was taller and bigger than both my brothers. Luckily for them, I had no thirst for revenge. I was only interested in my size and appearance for one reason: I wanted a girlfriend.

One day that summer, I was walking to the store when I saw Katie, a girl I'd known for years, riding her bike toward me. She was riding slowly, doubling her friend—who was one of the most gorgeous girls I'd ever seen. She was blonde, as I was, with a slim figure and all the right parts in all the right places. Katie stopped in front of me. "Hi, Spence," she said. Her friend, still perched on the bike seat, smiled at me over Katie's shoulder. "This is Emily," said Katie. "Want to come to the mall?"

By the end of the day, I had my first real girlfriend. Emily and I only lasted for a few weeks, but they were weeks I'd never forget. When we broke up, we agreed that the relationship had been mostly physical, since we were so attracted to each other.

"I think I've been using you," she said.

"I know what you mean," I said sadly.

I was secretly delighted by our breakup talk. This beautiful girl counted me in the same league as her, and couldn't get to know me because she was too distracted by my looks. *Mostly physical!* I had never even kissed a girl until I met Emily. My confidence soared. With my junior high gang going to a different high school, I would turn a new page, I told myself.

Please let me find good people, I said in my prayers. *And let me find a way to support myself. Don't let me end up in debt like my parents. Please lead me to a family and a good life, and protect the health of those I love. And please send me someone to love.*

Whoever heard my prayers was, of course, far wiser than I. What He knew, that I didn't, was that, at fourteen years old, I was immature and naïve, and far from ready to love or be loved by any girl.

I never prayed to be good looking, or even thanked God for this blessing in my prayers, but I was aware of it. All through the first year of high school, I pursued the prettiest girls. I asked them out. Some turned me down, but many said yes. A month or a week—or a day—later, we were tired of each other and I moved on. There was never any genuine connection. But at the beginning of grade ten, I met the girl of my dreams. I walked into my Foods class and a pretty girl with long brown hair caught my eye. I sat down beside her. I watched her lean over her schedule, her hair tucked behind her ear. I could see, in her neat handwriting, that she filled her after-school hours with sports. I introduced myself, and she smiled. She said her name was Anna.

By the end of class that day, I knew Anna was perfect for me. We came from different sides of the spectrum when it came to interests and background, but she had this element of grace to her that I fell in love with, and as I got to know her, my conviction and admiration grew. She was fit and studious and liked to have fun, but didn't drink excessively or use a lot of drugs. The only problem was that she already had a boyfriend. She and I used to talk on the phone for hours, and I was always respectful of her relationship—even though, in the back of my mind, I knew I was just biding my time.

One Friday in grade eleven, Anna came up to me in the hallway and grabbed my crotch. She said, "It's touchy-feely day!"

"My favourite day," I said, tussling with her. This was different. She'd never touched me before. Well, not like that, and openly, in the school hallway.

I wanted to crush her into a hug and kiss her right there. Instead I said, "Are you coming to my party tonight?"

"Sure!"

I had no idea what was going on. She never came to our parties. Something had changed, and I liked it.

That evening, I tried to spend time with Anna, but I was attempting to protect my house at the same time—my parents were often home when we had parties, but this time they were out of town, and things were getting out of control. Reagan was hanging out with his girlfriend, Kelly, and Craig was having too much fun to care whether anything got wrecked, so I had a hard time giving Anna the attention she deserved. Around midnight, I helped her into her coat and said I'd walk her to her car. We stepped outside holding hands, but we didn't make it halfway down the driveway before a fight broke out.

"Hey!" I said, pulling the two guys apart. They were so drunk, I couldn't figure out why the fight had started. I don't think they knew themselves. I finally convinced them both to leave, in opposite directions. Anna was waiting for me by her car.

"Sorry," I said.

"That's okay," she smiled, shaking her head a bit. I knew these parties weren't really her scene. I was beginning to feel like they weren't mine either.

"I'm glad you came," I said.

"Me, too."

"But I'd rather be alone with you." I put my arms around her.

"Sometime soon."

With that sweet promise between us, Anna and I had our first kiss. It was worth waiting for over a year.

All weekend, I looked forward to seeing her at school. On Monday, we sat together in class, but when I brushed against her arm, she pulled away and said, "Hi, Spence," and acted like nothing had happened.

A mutual friend told me Anna and her boyfriend had broken up the week before, only to get back together on Sunday.

If she and I had dated, my life probably would have changed for the better; with her influence, I would have found new friends and would likely have turned away from drugs and partying and focused more on my future. But we were destined just to be friends. I played along and pretended nothing had happened between us, but I would never sell the memory of that kiss.

My other big crush was Lindsey. She was one of the prettiest girls in school, and though she was never my girlfriend, and we never even kissed, Lindsey was, in a way, the only girl I ever dated. By that I mean we went on dates—I took her to the zoo and to the movies. Lindsey, like Anna, had a boyfriend, and considered me a close friend. I even taught her how to work the clutch in my parents' standard transmission car.

Around then I developed my theory that *all the good girls were taken.* I believed that for years, and it led me into a bit of trouble. At one point, a guy from a different school was hanging around outside my classes waiting for me because I'd been giving a girl he was dating a bit too much attention. Luckily, he showed up while I was at his school, looking for him. Eventually, that situation led to a fight, and I broke a bone in my hand against that guy's face. The girl of our mutual affections lost interest in both of us.

As I partied my way through high school, looking in vain for love, Reagan grew up fast. He'd started dating Kelly when they were sixteen, and by the time they were seventeen, Kelly was pregnant. The choice was clear: Reagan and Kelly got married before Dylan was born that April, and my brother found a job so he could support his new family. I wanted to get married young, too, but I saw how much work it was to have a child without first establishing a profession. Reagan had always been an introspective, somewhat cynical person, and I think all his responsibilities exaggerated those personality traits. He always did everything young, and Dylan would follow in his father's footsteps, fathering his own daughter at seventeen.

"I'm a grand-dude," Reagan would say. "That's what it's called when you're still in your thirties."

Back in high school, Craig seemed to take all our family's drama in stride. He was charismatic, cheerful, and the luckiest guy I knew; he skated through life on luck. When we were little, he'd find twenty-dollar bills lying in the street. Craig was always fun and pleasant to be around, just like our father. He could make anyone laugh. In fact, Craig was so easygoing, no one ever worried about him, including me, and it was only years later that I realized my brother felt pain and anger just like anyone else.

I, on the other hand, was never one to retreat. I felt my parents had become increasingly preoccupied with their own friends and interests, often leaving us to fend for ourselves in the evenings, and I reacted loudly. Maybe it was just the personality I was born with, but more than anything, I craved attention, and the less I found it at home, the more I sought it at school and in my social life. Once again, I demonstrated how far a person would go to fulfill his greatest desire—and, with my tall, muscular frame, dimples, blond hair, and booming voice, I was good at catching eyes. Walking down the street, I flashed a charming smile at every attractive girl I saw. In every room I entered, I joked loudly, flirted outrageously (even one of my surgeons at the U of A Hospital, years later, would call me a "pathological flirt"), and demanded the spotlight. When I did jobs for my dad, I topped all the workers with my raunchy jokes and friendly abuse. People loved to party with me because I always took charge and made sure everyone was entertained. I had the perfect disposition for cocaine, which cranked my personality to an all-time, attention-getting high.

Still, although I wasn't exactly introspective then, I did have my quiet contemplative moments. One of my favourite activities was camping, and I was always the guy in charge of the campfire, holding a stick to constantly readjust the logs and keep the fire going. I spent many nights mesmerized by the flames as they jumped and flickered up toward the sky. It was there that I wondered what life held for me after high school. Should I really join the family business? Both my brothers had other plans. Was there something else I was meant to do? Was there more to life than increasing my income so that I could maximize my partying potential? Was I capable of laying groundwork more important than that inside new suburban houses? When I returned home, I soon forgot all about these thoughts. They only stayed as I stared at the embers changing colour, cascading from red to orange, black, and then red again. Then the sparks floated away in the air, each dying out before landing.

• • •

Whyte Avenue

With high school almost over, I considered my options. I'd always loved cooking, I was good with numbers and accounting, and I was renowned for the parties I planned.

"You're so good at talking," my friend Anna joked. "Maybe you could get people to pay you for it."

"Your best option is to finish your training as a floor layer," my dad told me. I knew he was right. I needed a job, and I already had a specialized skill. I'd been training since I was eight years old.

"Even most of the people that do it can't do it right," Dad sighed.

I knew what he was talking about. He'd always had a hard time finding good workers, and often came home with stories of new employees who'd seemingly never touched flooring before in their lives. Floor laying, unlike most of the other trades, was still taught by apprenticeship instead of in colleges. This was good news for families like mine, where perfectionist fathers passed their skills on to perfectionist sons. The downside was that people with little skill or care could easily get into the business, though without finesse and dexterity, they never lasted long. I thought of the time my father's entire crew showed up to an important job drunk, and he had to send them all home. He wasn't kidding when he said he needed me.

I started working at my father's company halfway through my last year of high school. At the end of April, when I had two months left of high school, business picked up even more. I loved the work and collected an impressive paycheque every couple of weeks. I calculated how much more I'd earn if I were working full-time, and the choice was clear.

I was only taking two courses, and I needed to pass one to graduate, so I went to my teachers and said, "My dad really needs me for his company. Do you mind if I miss the last two months of school? I'll write my finals, and whatever score I get is what grade I get."

They both agreed. I think they'd always known I would be a tradesperson, and saw no reason to stand in my path. I took my exams in June with everyone else and finished with a 49 in English and a 51 in math. I got my diploma, and while some of my friends had their pre-college flings that summer, I was already a working man.

I spent eight to twelve hours each workday laying floors with one of my dad's installers, Al. I bought my first car—a white Cavalier. The first time I drove it, I cruised down Whyte Avenue, the hub of Edmonton's nightlife, with my friend Ralph, and he puked down the side of my new ride.

I was usually stoned and spent my weekends high on cocaine. I was so good at hiding it that my parents never realized I was into drugs, even though I still lived with them. Life felt pretty good until I clued in that, every two weeks, I used my paycheque to cover the insurance on my car, and there was nothing left. The rest was going to drinking and to my increasingly extravagant drug habit. I also didn't meet a lot of people, since I spent my time in the same few St. Albert bars, and in my drug dealer's living room.

I finally knew I had a serious problem, and I knew what it was. I even knew how to fix it: stop doing drugs. That sounds easy enough, but the problem went deeper than even physical craving. I'd built my entire social life around pot and cocaine. I couldn't leave them behind without leaving all my friends. Everyone I knew was into coke, acid, weed, mushrooms, or worse, and every time I socialized, getting high was on the agenda. And it was fun, but fun was no longer worth what that lifestyle was doing to my ambition, desires, and my time. Not to mention my bank account. My party habits were eating away all those things. Plus, as I watched my friends experiment more and more, I didn't want to do those more dangerous drugs.

My need to be liked, my need for attention, hadn't faded. Once again, the incredible force of that need exerted itself over my life. The easiest way to fulfill our needs almost always turns out to be a trap, and with drugs, the easy answer was to fall deeper into a self-destructive lifestyle. The only real solutions I could see were to figure out why I was doing so much coke, to change my friends, to quit. Of course, the person I was hurting most was myself, and in my more thoughtful moments, I knew I was leaving myself no potential for personal growth. I prayed for a way out of my trap.

My drug dealer back then was my friend Rick. I drove up to his house one day after work and parked in an empty spot on the driveway. An hour later, I was sitting on the dusty couch with my feet beside an empty pizza box and a beer in my hand, chatting with a couple of friends—there were always "friends" in that house—when a stocky, muscular guy I'd never seen before stepped in the door and glared.

"Which of you is in my parking spot?" he yelled. He looked ready to tear someone's head off. The guy wasn't huge, but I didn't want to mess with him. "Whose. Cavalier. Is on. My driveway."

"Um," I said. "I guess that's mine." He stared, and I stood up. "I'll just move it," I offered.

"This is my new roommate," said Rick, stepping in from the kitchen with a pot of mac and cheese in one hand. "Jay. Jay, this is Spence."

“That is disgusting, man,” said Jay, eyeing the fork sticking straight out of Rick’s bright orange meal.

Some introduction.

That Friday evening, I was watching TV after dinner when the doorbell rang.

“You have a guest,” my mom called to me.

I had no idea who it might be, so I glanced in the mirror, ran a hand through my hair, which I was growing out to ponytail length, and headed down the stairs. I’m not sure what I was hoping for, but it definitely wasn’t Jay standing solidly in the middle of the doorway. Rick must have given him my address. I said hello a little warily.

“Hey, Spence,” he said. “I’m heading to Malibu. Do you want to come?”

“Malibu?”

“Club Malibu. On Whyte Ave. Come on; let’s go fire it up.” That was to become our party saying.

“Okay,” I said slowly. “Just give me a minute.” He stepped inside, and I heard him chatting politely with my mother as I put on a tee-shirt and jeans. I heard him telling her that he worked on the oil rigs up north and would be heading back in a few weeks.

As we drove into Edmonton in his Jeep, I learned that we had a lot in common, with some exceptions. He liked to have a good time, but none of his money went up his nose.

“I’m not into coke,” he said. “I’ve never touched drugs and I never will.” As Jay saw it, drugs were a waste of precious time and money, and that was that. He had better things to do. Like drink. A lot.

Club Malibu was an unassuming-looking brick building just off the main strip, with a non-stop party inside. We walked through the lineup, and the bouncer, who allowed us in without question, immediately greeted Jay like an old friend. Inside, a slim, black-haired waitress stopped to hug Jay. Before I knew what was happening, there was a drink in my hand and half a dozen girls at our table. We were still at the club after it closed, sitting in the back room with waitresses on our laps, talking about which after-hours party they should take us to. It was a whole new world for me, and a fun one.

That night, Jay drove me out of the suburbs, away from the lure of Rick's wares, and away from nights spent stoned out of my mind in front of the TV. Jay and I spent many weekend and weekday nights on Whyte Ave after that, and I left my old friends almost completely. I'd finally found a friend who wasn't into that lethal cocktail of drugs and lethargy. And to think I met him in my drug dealer's living room. Of course, Jay wasn't perfect, and neither was my life. We were both enthusiastic drinkers, and I continued to smoke pot. Still, quitting cocaine gave me newfound clarity and increased the money I saved to an extent that shocked me. Jay was my only friend who made and saved more money than I did. He'd be gone for weeks, working up north, and then, out of the blue, I'd get a phone call.

"I'm on my way into town," Jay would say. "We're going out."

"But I have to work tomorrow."

"I don't care!"

I didn't take a lot of convincing. We both had cash to spend, and we'd stay out at Club Malibu or Barry T's until 3:00 A.M. and then get a late-night bite to eat. I went to work tired and hung over the next day, and then we'd go out again the next night. Jay was a good and an adventurous friend, but an exhausting one! No wonder he wasn't into cocaine—he didn't need any chemically induced energy or charisma.

During those nights in the clubs with Jay, I found I could pick up any girl as long as I was brave enough to ask. And talking to girls was not a problem for me. Partying with Jay, I changed my attitude that all the good girls were taken and decided that the best girls were waitresses. After all, they were usually the prettiest girls in the bar, and I found a vast majority of them were single. They were so used to getting hit on, I knew I needed an "A" game to succeed in acquiring their phone numbers. I was up for the challenge, and it wasn't long before I'd met and even dated several of the waitresses at our favourite bars.

"I just stick to my rules," I told Jay. "First of all, never be afraid of girls. If you can't get up and introduce yourself, it's a non-starter. Second, never forget a girl's name. When you get a girl's name and forget it, never go back. The third rule is, always have money in your pocket and always buy her a drink." Waitresses would drink on the job, but it had to be a shooter, because they didn't have time for anything else.

Meanwhile, I still prayed to find true love. It may seem obvious that I was going about finding it in the worst possible way, but all my short-term successes with women helped build my confidence just as I longed for a more meaningful relationship. I wasn't afraid to approach women, speak to them, or use all my tricks to charm them, plus I had killer dimples. But I still suffered my high school dilemma. My relationships fizzled out as quickly as they began. Often a "relationship" lasted as long as it took to grope a bit on a dance floor. I started to think maybe all the good girls weren't those with boyfriends and weren't waitresses either. Maybe all the good ones were those I could find things in common with. I'd been pursuing girls as attention seeking as I was; girls who turned heads, but cared more about their own egos than in connecting in a genuine way. I wanted someone with depth, someone caring and decent. And sexy, too—I hadn't given up on that requirement!

Then one night at Barry T's, I noticed a woman I hadn't seen before. She was tall and pretty, but not flashy, with long blonde hair. As she walked past me, heading for the back of the bar, I tapped her on the shoulder.

"Want to dance?" I asked.

I thought things were going great. I mimicked the other dancers and showed her my silliest moves, and I saw that she had a slow smile that brightened her face. When she disappeared at the end of the song, I wondered what I'd done wrong. I only learned later that I'd intercepted her on her way to the lady's room.

That blonde woman reappeared on the dance floor, and we danced together for the whole night. I asked for her phone number, and when I unfolded the scrap of paper later, at home, I saw a number and three names: Sammy, Tina, and Terence. Luckily, remembering a girl's name was one of the first entries in my dating rule book. Plus I never forgot things, even when I was drinking. I phoned Tina two days later. Within six months, we were living together, and three years later, we were married.

• • •

Tina

After one of my presentations in 2008, during my usual question period, a man in coveralls, holding his hardhat on his lap, put his hand up. "You have an amazing story here," he said, "but I think half the story is missing. What about your wife? How did she cope? What did she go through? How has the fire affected her?" I heard murmurs of agreement through the crowd. And this was nothing new; people always wanted to know about Tina. Even the people close to us had trouble understanding what she'd gone through, because she never complained, never talked about herself.

"I agree with you," I said. "My wife went through even more stress than I did, and as my plastic surgeon always said, she's the real hero in this situation. But these presentations aren't really her thing. She's a very private person." I didn't know then that our marriage was already in trouble.

• • •

When I first met Tina, I could see she was different from the other girls I'd been chasing. Of course she was beautiful, as that was a must for me back then, but her beauty was different from what I was used to. She wasn't wearing revealing clothes, and didn't have her hair all stuck in place with a can of hairspray. Her makeup wasn't so thick you would need a professional solvent to remove it. She was just naturally beautiful.

Since the day I met Tina, she was committed and devoted to me. She was loving and kind, and she was amazingly generous with herself. I was swept off my feet by her, and over the years I came to know someone irreplaceable. As we grew up together, she became even more beautiful throughout her twenties and into her thirties. But more important, she was humble, reserved, and she had a pure heart full of compassion and love. She is very pretty on the outside, but she is drop-dead gorgeous on the inside.

Tina and I never dated; we went straight into a relationship. God had finally sent me the right girl, and there didn't seem any reason to wait. I wanted it, she wanted it, and we just matched. It wasn't long before her roommate insisted I start paying rent. Tina worked at a clothing store back then, and then she moved to the newspaper call centre, dealing with complaints. That she spent her days absorbing other people's complaints and still had enough care and compassion for all her friends and me illustrates the depth of her kindness.

For two years, Tina and I lived together, and though she was happy to continue that way, I was uncomfortable with it. I hadn't attended church regularly for a few years, but my faith was important to me. I knew I could be excommunicated for living with Tina without marrying her, but I loved her and knew she was the woman I wanted to spend the rest of my life with. I understood Tina's uncertainty about marriage, especially since her parents had divorced when she was a child. Part of me was scared as well—although I'd longed for true love all my life, "forever" suddenly seemed like an extremely long time.

We struggled with the tension between my religious convictions, our mutual fear of commitment, and Tina's skepticism about marriage until two years into our relationship. When we were both twenty-three, Tina was hospitalized and needed surgery. She was fine, but the incident scared me, and I remember sitting beside her hospital bed, wanting to propose right there. I wanted to show that I was serious; I wanted to publicly, verbally commit to the woman I loved.

Shortly after that, I went ring shopping with Jay and his girlfriend, who also worked with Tina, and I bought an eternity band. Technically, that ring was a wedding band. I didn't know that engagement rings were usually set with a single stone. We often went to football games—I'd turned her into an Edmonton Eskimos fan even though to this day she doesn't understand the rules—so I planned to propose at the home opener against Toronto. I planned the day carefully, and twenty close friends who always went to the games were in on it.

An hour into the game, my proposal still hadn't appeared on the screen, and Tina was freezing, shifting uncomfortably in her seat. She was looking everywhere but at the field.

"It's a good game," I kept insisting. "I don't want to leave partway!" It clearly was not a good game, but Tina accepted my obsession to see it through, even when it started raining.

"I'll be right back," Tina said, partway through the second quarter.

"Where are you going?"

She gestured toward the washroom.

"Okay," I said, "but hurry up!"

Tina gave me a funny look and walked away. While she was gone, I showed the ring to my friends, and it fell and started rolling on the concrete. Luckily, my buddy stopped it just in time. I was shoving the box back into my pocket as Tina paused to brush some rainwater off her seat before sitting down.

Finally, near the end of the third quarter, my words appeared on the big screen: "Tina, will you marry me?" I kneeled in a puddle of water and beer, and the Edmonton Eskimos Club, to my surprise, presented Tina with a bouquet of flowers.

"Yes," she said. "I'll marry you." She laughed as I slipped the ring onto her finger and she hugged me tightly. All our friends cheered.

I was relieved and excited—but a bit perplexed. Tina didn't seem quite as surprised as I'd expected. I'd hoped for at least a tear or two of joy. A few days later, she finally admitted she'd overheard me planning the proposal on the phone. She'd known about it the whole time, and had even held off on going to the washroom for as long as she could during the game, in case she missed the big event. Just like on the night we met, she had to ignore nature's call while I tried my hardest to charm her.

"It's not my fault," she kidded me. "You just talk so loud!"

A year later, we were married in Tina's hometown of Slave Lake, Alberta. Tina's background was Catholic, though she and her mother had never been churchgoers. We had the Lutheran pastor from St. Albert marry us in a Catholic church. The 130 guests at our wedding included my childhood best friend, now nicknamed Redwood because of his massive legs, as my best man, and Jay, Rick, and Craig. Our friends said it was the best wedding they'd ever been to, even though things didn't go quite as planned. In fact, if things could go wrong they did! It started the night before the wedding, when one of my best men dropped out, and, as a last ditch effort, I asked my brother Craig to step in. Luckily, the tux fit him, but, unfortunately, Craig was in party mode back then, and didn't stop until late in the evening. By the time the wedding happened, he was so hung over he could barely stand. He had sweat pouring down his face during the ceremony and I thought he was going to throw up.

Then, during the ceremony, I accidentally put out my right hand to receive the ring, so all the pictures show me covering my finger, trying to hide my little error, so now we have a bunch of wedding pictures where it looks like I'm not wearing a ring at all. After we signed the marriage certificate and walked out of the church, I realized that my right finger was bigger than my left, and I couldn't get the ring off. Luckily, Jay got me some soap, and after lubricating my finger he helped me pull off the ring. Finally, for the banquet, Tina had made two connecting hearts with our names on them and placed them at the head table where she and I were supposed to sit, but we ended up entering the room in the wrong order and sat behind the wrong names.

Then the fun began. I, of course, drank too much because I was having so much fun celebrating our union with all the people I cared about. Tina let go of her shyness that night to show her wild side, and at the end of the night, she and I were the last to leave. My romantic plans were thwarted when we had to call her mom to come and unbutton Tina's dress; the many tiny buttons were just too small for my fingers. Then, in the morning, I threw up from all the drinking I'd done, which was out of character for me.

All in all, it was a perfect wedding. Two people who loved each other were wed, had fun, and shared the moment with 130 close friends and family members. Tina and Spencer Beach started their new life together. And oh yeah—it poured rain that day, too! Tina and I used to joke that we were jinxed. Whenever we made plans, it rained or I got hurt. "Those are the jinxes we have to live with in return for our lovely marriage," I told her.

Miraculously, however, we avoided both rain and injury on our honeymoon. We drove to Vancouver and Victoria, following the sun. We had a warm, clear trip, and each evening when we checked the weather forecast, we saw that the rain was a day behind us. I wish I could have given her a better honeymoon but neither of us came from privileged families, so we had to pay for the vast majority of the wedding. We could only afford the honeymoon due to some cash gifts we received at the gift opening. We were young, broke, and in love.

• • •

Top Floor

The first years of my marriage with Tina were good and also challenging. I was determined to be a strong provider, and in my mind that meant working as hard as I could, as much as I could. I was still working for my father at Beach Brothers. Every morning, I got up at six, and I wouldn't get home until sometime between six and ten o'clock at night. That's how I was raised—to be the "big guy." I was obsessed with staying out of debt, and every extra hour I worked was that much extra money in the bank. Plus, I loved what I did. There was nothing I'd have rather been doing than working with my hands. I still wasn't going to church regularly. I was just too busy, I told myself. I couldn't take the time.

There was a lot of pressure on me, because I was the only Beach of my generation following in the family business. Reagan was busy with his family and training as a graphic designer, and Craig opted for a more laid-back existence, delivering pizzas. The customers, my dad, and my grandfather all expected me to be the best installer because I was a Beach, but I didn't know more than anyone else did. I worked hard and, luckily, picked up concepts quickly. I found I could rise to the top by amalgamating the techniques I learned from everyone around me, and by creating tricks of my own.

The same qualities that make me a good speaker today helped me excel at my flooring work: I always strove for perfection, and I wasn't afraid to tear things apart and redo them. I never left visible seams in carpeting or ruined a flight of stairs. For some reason I'll never understand, flooring guys often struggle with that one. I didn't show up to work drunk, either, but I did show up stoned. Back then, I was stoned almost all the time; I could barely imagine what the world would look like if I left the house without the benefit of a few tokes. Tina didn't do any drugs, and she didn't realize just how big a part of my life they had become. She never questioned me about how much I spent on dope, but I am sure deep down she would have rather had a holiday instead of a stoned husband!

The year after Tina and I were married, 1998, I bought into the Beach Brothers to become part owner. The next year, the company succumbed to economic pressures, and went under. Sadly for Craig, he'd chosen the worst moment to quit driving pizzas and start laying floors with us. For a few months, we were still working for our dad but weren't getting paid, so when I ran out of cash, I used my RRSPs to help Tina pay the rent in our rundown apartment with its leak, which the landlord refused to fix, right in the bedroom. The next month, the night before our rent was due, Tina and I lay in bed, which was now in the living room.

"I'm sorry," I said. I was supposed to provide for my family, and I was failing miserably.

"It's not your fault," replied Tina.

But I couldn't just sit there doing nothing.

We held each other for a minute, minds racing over how to get out of our predicament. I kissed Tina's hair and then I turned and kissed the wall.

Tina laughed. "What are you doing?"

"Kissing this place goodbye."

We packed all night and left that apartment before the sun came up, leaving no trace and certainly no cash. We showed up with all our things at the apartment of two guys I worked with. I knew they were looking for a roommate, and now they had two. Tina hated that place, especially since one of our new roommates had a pet snake. I started working for other companies to pay the bills, and within a month, Tina found us a better place to live. I gradually stopped working for my father altogether. It was the only way I could support myself. Beach Brothers had run its course.

Meanwhile, my mother supported herself and my father with her farmers' market business while Dad went through the motions of bankruptcy and took a little while to re-examine his options. Then my father did what he'd always dreaded: he agreed to work for a boss. And that boss was my mother. While she pickled vegetables and administrated several farmers' markets, my father perfected his jams and marmalades, and they set up booths in malls throughout the city. He'd always loved to cook, and it wasn't long before this new career became more lucrative than flooring ever was.

"I never thought I'd be doing this," my dad said, with his characteristic good-hearted ease. "But I'm happy." He was on his own time, and no one talked back to him. Best of all, he didn't have to rely on anyone who might prove unreliable. He found himself happy to say goodbye to all the logistics and headaches of the flooring business, and his wares eventually became renowned.

My father had always told me not to worry about the future—there's no way to know what will happen tomorrow; only God knows that. We can only plan for the best, and prepare for the fact that all our plans might change. As my father and I can both attest, there's no point worrying about future contingencies. They're out of our hands. Luckily, they're in the hands of someone much more capable.

• • •

But after Beach Brothers's collapse, I wasn't thrilled with my daily life. I knew I was a good worker, with better skills than most people in the business, and I never had trouble finding work. But flooring could be a dirty business. It was easy for unscrupulous small-business owners to get away with cutting corners, and some bosses didn't play fair. For instance, it was illegal to make employees pay their own Workers' Compensation Board insurance, but many contracts I signed included a deduction for "coffee expenses"—and that coffee happened to cost exactly the same as workers' comp. I paid a few hundred dollars every month for that "coffee." I'd had it good working for my father. I hadn't realized what an outstanding boss he had been.

Then my friend Grant, who'd also been working for my father, found employment with a company called Top Floor, and he recommended me to his boss, Jack.

"You're in," Grant told me. He said Jack was a fair boss, but trusted people about as far as he could throw them. "And if you screw up, you're out of there. He fires people all the time."

"Fine with me."

In time, firing people would become one of my jobs, and the guys on the crew would call me the "Axe Man."

Jack was a charming man with greying hair and wide eyes. Grant was right that Jack didn't have any qualms about firing someone who wasn't working out, but I did work out, and because I was a good worker, Jack was a great boss. I recommended Craig, and Jack hired him, too.

For once, I didn't have to pay for supplies or for my own helper. I received a good hourly wage, and there were no "coffee expenses" deducted from my pay. Finally, I didn't have to fight and haggle for work. Each morning, we all met at a warehouse, where we picked up our job supplies for the day, and Jack doled out the work. Along with Craig, and Grant, and me, there were some great guys on that crew, including Vail, whose parents owned the company Jack contracted from. Vail became a good friend of mine. Our crew was close-knit; we helped each other out when the jobs were big or complicated, and we shared techniques with each other. I couldn't have asked for more. Jack gave me my work, I did what I was told, and then I went home.

For my first job with Top Floor, I went to a new house with two rolls of carpet in my truck. I walked through the house and read the order. I was supposed to carpet the family room in one colour, and the bonus room in another. The house had two rooms, one upstairs and one downstairs, that looked essentially the same to me. I walked back and forth between them, trying to guess what a "bonus room" might be. I had never heard the term before. I took a guess and got to work.

I botched that first job. My guess was wrong. It turns out a bonus room is an extra room above the garage, usually without a closet, that can be used as a den or rec room. Who knew?

"We're going to have to rip out all that carpet and start again," Jack said.

"I'm sorry," I said. "I didn't know."

"Well, why didn't you ask?"

Good question. I didn't really have an answer.

"Did you know that Thomas Edison tried thousands of methods of harnessing electricity for light before he invented the light bulb?" Jack said.

I didn't.

"And do you know what he said when he hit on one that worked? He said he hadn't made ten thousand mistakes; he'd just found ten thousand ways that didn't work."

"Right ..." I said.

"You see what I'm getting at, Spence? It's okay to make a mistake. Now you know what a bonus room is, right?"

I did.

"But next time, if you don't know something, just ask."

Jack was right. There was no good reason to have guessed in this situation—finding the bonus room wasn't quite on a par with inventing the light bulb!

"It's okay to admit that you were wrong."

I nodded.

"So, admit it."

"Yeah ..."

"Spence, just admit that you were wrong."

He wasn't going to let up.

"Okay," I said. "I was wrong."

Despite screwing up my first job, I was soon one of Top Floor's best workers. Most floor layers choose one kind of flooring; my dad was a linoleum expert like his father, and some guys do carpet or ceramic, or hardwood and laminate. I had learned all aspects of the trade, and I had all my own tools.

We worked alone or in pairs, but often all the workers would go out for a beer in the evening. As at all workplaces, we liked to hear funny stories about our boss, and Grant had a great one about ours. Jack drove a blue extended Dodge work van—luxury was his style—and the most noticeable thing about his van was its vanity plate: K-BOOM.

"What's up with Jack's licence plate?" I asked one day, after work.

Grant told me Jack once burned down a trailer while working with a solvent called Roberts 1901, which we often used to dissolve the adhesive that held lino to subflooring. He'd had his vanity licence plate made up to commemorate the event.

Then Grant told me about another contact fire during an installation. Jack's business partner at the time had run out of the house and down the street in his socks. "It was hilarious!" Grant said. I had to laugh. I guess everyone likes to hear funny stories about the boss's screw-ups. Hell, the picture in my head was even funnier than any clip I had watched on *America's Funniest Videos.*

• • •

For almost three years, my wife and I led a content, routine life, with no major incidents. My family was doing well. Reagan and Kelly now had three sons—Dylan, Tyler, and Ryan—and Reagan was working as a graphic designer for the municipal government. We all celebrated Craig's marriage to Sandra, a strong, smart woman who loved my brother enough to be called "Sandy Beach" for the rest of her life.

I was content. When I prayed at night, I always said, "Thank you for this beautiful day." I said that whether the day had been sunny or grey, easy or frustrating. I always said, "Please let me have another beautiful day tomorrow. Thank you for protecting my family." After the fire, I saw how every day back then was beautiful—more beautiful than I realized at the time. Everything in life I'd ever needed or prayed for, I had.

The guys I worked with spent a lot of time at the bar, and so did I. Of course, I no longer went out looking for love, but I did sometimes use my "rules" to bring girls to our table, where they could meet my single friends. I had a good time with those guys, but I was ready for the next stage of my life. Being a parent couldn't be easy—I suspected that every parent screwed up in some major way—but I was eager to get started on a family. Tina wasn't so sure, and needed more time to get her own life on track. I have to admit, it wasn't easy for me to be patient. I knew Tina found her job unfulfilling, and I made enough to support both of us, so I found it difficult to understand why she didn't want to take a maternity leave—maybe a permanent one.

As I contemplated having children of my own, I talked to my parents about some leftover resentment from my youth. They apologized and explained their point of view. They knew they'd made mistakes, and when I imagined myself in their shoes, I could understand how they'd made them. Of course, I still feel twinges of frustration sometimes—who doesn't, toward their parents?—but I firmly believe that if people at least try to rectify their mistakes, forgiveness should be instant. If you don't forgive, you're the one making the next huge, terrible mistake. It's one of my life's strangest ironies that Jack was the first to teach me that lesson, since he was the person whose mistakes would mark me, most obviously, forever.

• • •

A Long Way Down

For the August long weekend in 2002, Tina and I planned a trip to Ram Falls, near the town of Rocky Mountain House. We'd been there before, and it was one of the nicest falls in the Alberta Rockies. The last time we'd gone there, our friend had lost his camera tripod in Hummingbird Falls, a triple falls that we renamed Tripod Falls. We also went horseback riding, and when my horse decided to take a shortcut to the creek we were to cross, it ran me through a pine tree, then jumped off a drop into the stream where I hurt myself on the saddle's stirrup. The horse was named Gizmo, and I renamed him Jizmo because of where he hurt me. It was a fun trip though; I never let a few little accidents ruin my good time.

Tina was reluctant to go, because it gets cold at night in the mountains and she hates the cold. "You're going to love it," I told her that Friday morning. I just had to finish a small bathroom with vinyl tile, and then we could leave until Monday night. "I won't be long," I said, as I left the house. "If you finish packing, I'll be back by the time you're done."

I drove to the commercial building. It was a forty-five-minute job, but I knew I could finish it in closer to thirty minutes if I focused. All I could think about was getting on the road and leaving work behind for almost four days. I could practically smell the mountain air already. I'd take Tina to the McDonalds we always went to near Jasper, and I planned to order the Big Mac meal.

When I got to the job, I worked quickly to get set up. After unloading all my tools and material, I stepped out of the washroom and looked around for somewhere to plug in my vacuum cleaner. I was on the second storey of a mezzanine, but the floor hadn't been completed, so I was at the edge of a twelve-foot drop. I could see all the way down to the concrete ground. The furnace, sitting on the edge of the drop, towered up in front of me, and three feet past it, I could see the only electrical outlet. I'd have to lean over that precipice to plug in my vacuum.

I put one hand against the furnace, shoved, and tested its stability. It didn't budge. So with one arm braced against the furnace and the vacuum's cord in my other hand, I reached toward that outlet. Just as I put all my weight on the furnace, it began to twist. I had to think fast: the furnace was about to tip over with me under it. There was only one other option. I let go and jumped. As I fell, I thought, *As a kid I jumped from higher heights and survived. This is just a little drop!*

I landed on my feet, my knees buckled and my hands hit the unfinished floor. Immediately, I rolled onto my back to assess the damage, and the pain started to set in. I tried to lift my right leg so I could look at my ankle, and heard bones crunch. Agony tore into me. I stayed there on my back with my legs tucked into my chest and my arms around my knees, rocking slowly back and forth. A couple of things were clear. My ankles were screwed. My weekend was ruined.

I caught my breath, reached to my belt, and retrieved my cellphone, which was thankfully undamaged. I phoned Jack, and he sent Grant to pick me up. Easier said than done: he arrived quickly, but Grant had to heave me into his work van because I couldn't put any weight on my ankles. And I was a big man: six foot three and 170 pounds. Luckily, Grant was bigger. He made a joke as he hoisted me into his arms. Any good childhood friend knows that laughter is the best medicine.

Partway to the closest hospital, Grey Nuns, Grant told me, "Your ambulance needs gas," and pulled into a gas station.

"Just get five dollars' worth," I begged him.

When we finally got to the hospital, Grant went in to get help. Grey Nuns turned out to be a geriatric hospital, but instead of sending me on, they had me wait until all the elderly patients had been treated. In the waiting room, they put me in a wheelchair with my legs still supported by my arms wrapped around my knees, and Grant sat with me until Tina came.

"Why didn't you call an ambulance?" Tina asked.

"I called Jack."

"Why didn't Jack call an ambulance?"

"He didn't think it was that much of an emergency, I guess."

Tina didn't say anything.

Some of my other buddies from work came by to see me, and crowded into the little room I had finally been put in.

"You guys would use any excuse to get out of work," I said. "Now I'll have to work late to finish your jobs."

"I can't believe you're still joking around," Vail said.

Tina smiled. She knew I joked through everything. It was my way of coping.

All night, Tina rested on a gurney beside me as I waited in agony to be transferred to the University of Alberta Hospital, both of us trying not to dwell on the thought that an ambulance would have taken me straight there. We tried not to dwell on our lost trip to Ram Falls either.

"I told you we were jinxed," I said.

But after all, we did have each other. That always was enough. Ram Falls was just a place to be together.

In the early morning hours, I was transferred to a wheelchair and taken to the x-ray department. After the technician x-rayed my feet and ankles, I said, "You know, my wrist is really hurting me, too."

It turned out I'd broken both ankles and my left thumb. "You've also shattered your heel," the Emergency doctor told me. "That's bad news because the heel has no marrow. It's a bad bone to break. It shatters like an egg."

Then they casted me. I lay back with my legs up, and two nurses pushed my feet back until the casts set. After that ordeal, I finally got to ride in an ambulance to the University of Alberta Hospital. I needed surgery, but my ankles had swollen so much during my night in Emergency that the doctors said they'd have to wait. I had to wait in that hospital for a whole unbelievably boring week, watching my feet and lower legs turn dark purple, before the doctors could operate to screw in the steel plates that held my ankles together until they healed. Tina spent all her free time by my side, and we tried to keep each other entertained.

Those plates are still there to this day, with eleven long screws holding each one in. "You might always have a limp," the surgeon warned me after the operation. "You might not run again, and you might always suffer from some degree of pain."

I just looked that surgeon in the eye and knew he was mistaken. I knew I would get back to everything; there was no doubt in my mind. After all, I grew up with two brothers who had caused me more pain than this!

They kept me at the U of A Hospital for another two days, and then transferred me to the Glenrose Rehabilitation Hospital, an Edmonton facility that's North America's largest free-standing rehabilitation centre. For the first few days at the Glenrose, I just sat and stewed while they found me a physical therapist and fit me into their schedules. At the U of A, they had let me transfer myself from my bed into my wheelchair because my right arm was strong enough to handle my body weight, but at the Glenrose, they wouldn't. The surgeon said it was too dangerous. I became grumpier and grumpier about my lack of independence. I had to call a nurse for everything. I couldn't even move my wheelchair without help; my one-armed attempts just had me spinning in circles.

My parents and brothers visited me, and Tina kept coming every day. I also got a visit from my pastor, Dan Habben. My mother had phoned him when I was hurt, knowing he made a point of visiting injured and ill members of his congregation. I didn't know Pastor Habben well back then, because he'd only been at St. Peter's for three or four years, and he didn't know me at all, since I only attended services on holidays, when the church was packed. Maybe my mother saw an opportunity for our pastor to corner me while I couldn't run away. Pastor Habben was not much older than I was, and was married with a young family. He was plain-spoken though obviously intelligent and worldly—he was from the U.S. but grew up in Japan with missionary parents and spoke at least five languages. As we studied the Bible together, Pastor Habben and I got to know each other, and I discovered he was one of the best listeners I'd ever met. I respected and trusted him. He was friendly, caring, and thoughtful, and he knew just about everything about the Bible.

I wasn't listening too hard back then when Pastor Habben suggested, "Sometimes God slows us down for a reason—puts us flat on our backs so there's nowhere to look, for a while, but up at Him." Slowing down didn't appeal to me at all. I was just waiting to burst out of that wheelchair, out of that hospital, and back into my life. I didn't even slow down much during my stay; once they adjusted my wheelchair so I could turn both wheels with one hand, I was burning around the Glenrose, going to the gym and therapy, and socializing as much as humanly possible. Only later would it occur to me that all of it—the boring, painful hospital stay, the frustration of immobility, even rehab at the Glenrose—was a small taste of what would come.

Only a week and a half after I was admitted, I was in physiotherapy when I heard my name on the intercom: "Spencer Beach, please come to the nursing unit."

I wheeled out of the elevator and cruised down the hallway as fast as I could. The doctor was standing at the end of the hall as I sped toward him, wheeling with one hand. I braked to a sudden stop in front of him.

"What's up?" I said.

He looked me up and down. "You're going home today."

• • •

I went all the way back home—all the way to my parents' house in St. Albert. There was no way I could climb to the bedroom Tina and I shared on the second storey of our apartment. Tina visited me at my parents' place on the weekends. It was difficult to climb onto a bed with two broken feet and a broken hand, and my parents were using their extra bedrooms for canning, so we slept together on the living room floor.

My first cast came off after six weeks, but my heel took a couple of weeks longer to heal. The nurse who removed that second cast told me I wasn't ready to stand yet.

"Wait until you're at home with people around before you try. And take it easy. You haven't been on your feet for over two months."

That evening, in my parents' living room, I stood up, and fell backward onto the couch. My parents and Tina helped me to stand again.

It didn't take me long to walk with crutches, and I worked hard to get rid of those, too. I still had to go to physiotherapy, and I wasn't supposed to work until the Workers' Compensation Board said I was ready.

But a week or two after I shed my crutches Jack suggested I return to work.

"With your experience, I'll put you in a service position," he said.

"He's taking advantage of you," Tina said. She said he was pressuring me to go back before I was ready. I didn't see it that way. I was bored and restless, and I missed my work. My new position would come with freedom and control. I knew how to lay all the different kinds of flooring, but now had two broken feet and a broken bone in my hand. I could see Jack's reasoning. Service was a perfect fit. I also saw Tina's point, but I was eager to get back to work. Plus, we needed the money. The workers' comp payments just weren't enough.

Jack and I sealed the deal with a handshake and a smile.

He said, "With this raise and this new position, you take care of my problems."

My understanding of what he really meant was, *You follow orders, and in return, I'll take care of you. You'll have money in the bank, and a good life.* Sounded good to me.

I loved being Top Floor's service guy. I got to work on my own, I was paid more than anyone else, and I received a gas allowance. Since I was Jack's number-one guy, he treated me like gold. Around that time, Vail decided to stop working for Jack, so he was off his knees, and was working for his parents, instead. That made him Jack's boss: when people bought flooring from Vail's parents' company, they contracted the installation out to Jack, and then Jack apportioned the jobs to Gary, Grant, Al, Rayce, and his other employees. Finally, I showed up to fix the mistakes; I put out the fires, so to speak. Now, I didn't start out as a good teacher—I started out bossy and pompous. But I'm proud to say I became respectful and patient with the workers; by doing service work, I learned to figure out and explain where they'd gone wrong, so they could avoid making the same mistakes again.

I had a great relationship with the supplier, and I made customers happy because I was clean-cut, patient, and polite. I wasn't afraid to say, "This is damaged beyond my ability to fix it." I wasn't afraid to say, "Okay, I can fix this, but it's going to take half a day." Doing service, I learned the last things I needed to know about floor laying, and I developed such a name for myself, I had extra work almost every weekend. I trained myself to the point that I could have written a manual.

There was—and still is—no doubt in my mind that Jack and Vail's mentorships made me faster and better at my job; I respected Jack's expertise completely, and I never hesitated to adopt his ways of doing things. He just had better methods than I did. And I was always grateful that Jack had reminded me of the importance of humility, of recognizing the limits of my knowledge.

• • •

After my ankles healed, thanks in part to Pastor Habben's influence I started attending church regularly. It was difficult because I hadn't been there for so long. I knew the other congregants remembered me, though I didn't necessarily remember them, and I was afraid they'd think badly of me. But as Pastor Habben reminded me, church isn't a museum for saints, it's a hospital for sinners. My church family welcomed me back with open arms. I realized that whatever happened, St. Peter's would always be a safe place.

I resurrected the Pioneers, the church's Saturday children's group I'd attended growing up, because I loved spending time with kids, and it gave me a good excuse not to work on the weekends. I stopped partying completely—quit the bar scene cold turkey. My life was full with church, work, and my marriage, and I just didn't have time for that scene anymore. The change wasn't difficult; in fact, I barely thought about it. I'd drunk more alcohol than a fish has drunk water, and I'd had enough.

Tina and I were going through a bit of rough patch then, as she re-evaluated what marriage meant to her. Our friend Marc was engaged to a friend of Tina's, and she was thinking of leaving him. As their wedding drew closer and closer, there was more and more friction between them, and as our friends talked endlessly of their fears about marriage and relationships, Tina and I began to question whether all marriage was inherently doomed. Marc's situation somehow highlighted and exaggerated all the small tensions in our own relationship.

But then a wonderful thing happened. Tina told me she was pregnant. She'd already known for a few weeks.

"I didn't want to tell you until I was sure everything was okay," she said.

Impending fatherhood was one huge commitment that didn't scare me. Sure, I was nervous and didn't know what to expect, but far more than that, I was excited. I was so overjoyed, I couldn't keep the news to myself—which is probably part of the reason she didn't tell me right away. I started working harder than ever to prepare us financially. I was eager to grow up and be a family man and to raise my family in the church. I wanted to do things right for once in my life. Tina was happy, too, and it didn't hurt that before she asked for maternity leave, she was laid off. That was just fine with her. She could stop working at her frustrating job, still receive a paycheque for a while, and prepare for motherhood.

By late April 2003, Tina was four months pregnant. Marc and his girlfriend had gone through with their wedding but then broken up and divorced, and the negative effects of their relationship on ours were wearing off. Tina was a lot happier without her call-centre job, and we were both looking forward to getting started on our new adventure as parents. Life wasn't perfect, but it was pretty good, and, we thought, about to get better. Tina's doctor always referred to our future child as "the fetus," so I came up with the temporary name *Seba*. Seba Beach was a summer village outside of Edmonton. Tina and I loved the name, and it stuck until she gave birth.

• • •

For two days late that April, I showed up at the warehouse to get my service orders for the morning, knowing that my afternoon would be occupied with stripping lino that had been installed in the wrong colour from a new house in a development called Rutherford Close; the lino had been labelled as though correct, so another crew had installed it. The owners were planning to move in promptly, so the floors had to fixed immediately. Both days after lunch, I headed to that house with a fresh supply of Roberts 1901—the infamous "K-BOOM" solvent—determined to "get it done." I never looked forward to working with the stuff. It stank, and it made me feel dizzy and slightly nauseous, plus I could taste it for hours after the job was finished as I exhaled the chemical from my lungs throughout the evening. Jack called this assignment a "happy tub" because the chemical always made his workers light-headed. In fact, we used to phone our co-workers when we were good and high from the chemical, just for fun. This had become a tradition among all the workers in our crew.

I always began as Jack had told me, by turning down the furnace and opening the doors and windows. Although those were Jack's only precautions, I had additional rules: I never did this job in winter, since the house needed good ventilation, and I always insisted that young people leave while I was working. Knowing the fumes' effect on me, I was wary of what they might do to a child. In my gut I knew this chemical was dangerous, but so were other aspects of my job, and I had to provide for my family, I had to live up to my commitment to Jack. When I was told to strip lino, I knew I was expected to use his method with the solvent.

On the third morning, I woke up wishing I could avoid the fume-filled work ahead of me. I don't remember this, but Tina tells me I wanted to phone in sick. I never phoned in sick, not even when I was sick. Hell, I even went to work with half-healed ankles. It was a warm spring day, unseasonably warm for April 24.

"I love you," I said as I left, kissing Tina as she lay in bed, and I touched her belly to say goodbye to Seba, too. Tina was going to spend the day shopping for the baby.

All morning, I did service jobs and thought about my buddy Norris's stag party, which he'd asked me to plan. Since planning Marc's stag, I was known as the master. Some friends had asked me to throw them stags when they weren't even getting married, because Marc's was just that much fun. I enjoyed putting the events together, and that evening, I was going to sit down and sketch out the details. That was work I enjoyed as much as I disliked stripping lino with 901, as we called the chemical. As I finished up my last job before lunch, I told myself I'd eat, do the service job, and then have a relaxing evening planning the ultimate party.

I drove into Rutherford Close at one o'clock and got my tools together. I thought of reaching under my driver's seat for my leather work gloves, hesitated, and left them lying there. Who wants hot, sweaty hands when they're trying to work? And besides, gloves make it harder to manipulate tools, especially when those gloves are coated with a layer of reactivated glue.

I still had to strip the laundry room, a six-foot-long hallway, a half bathroom, and the front entry, and it would take a couple more hours. As always, I turned down the thermostat, then opened the windows, along with the front door and a door in the laundry room, which led to the garage. The garage itself was open to the street, and had no floor or stairs, so it was essentially a pit—a pit full of rubble, since that's where all the tradespeople had been told to dump their garbage. On top of the pile were large black garbage bags full of the lino I'd already stripped. There, I'd continue to throw the lino as I removed it.

There was only one other guy working in the house that day, a worker in his late forties whom I'd seen before when we worked on the same buildings. All the trades guys in town get to recognize each other eventually, but I didn't know his name, and we'd never spoken in depth. Tradespeople don't tend to intermingle; the less contact, the better, as far as the supervisors are concerned. We were there to "get 'er done," not to socialize. This guy and I chatted just enough for him to tell me he was installing shelves upstairs. I'd learn much later that his name was Richard.

I set a carton of four-litre 901 bottles on the floor. "Sorry about this stuff I'm using," I said. "It really stinks. You might want to open some windows up there."

Lino has four layers: the paper backing is glued firmly to the floor; the next layer is compact foam; on top of that is a layer embossed with a pattern; and finally that's topped with the wear layer, made of urethane. It was easy enough to rip up the top three layers, but that left all the backing stuck so firmly that scraping it up would wreck the plywood underneath, which would mean a day of filling in all the damage to the plywood before reinstalling the new product. That's where the 901 came in. Instead of damaging all the wood, I just poured on the chemical, waited a few minutes, and then peeled up the backing like a wet Band-Aid. The 901, designed to clean adhesive spills, transformed glue to a mildly sticky goop. This method worked so well, it even left intact all the floor layers' patch that we used to fill in the plywood seams.

The only problem was that the wood remained sticky with glue where I peeled off each sheet of backing, and even after scraping, a light residue remained. That's why I never jammed the doors open with wood, which would have stuck to the subfloor, wrecking the smooth surface I was so careful to create. I didn't want to use my hammers or other tools because they would become sticky, and then dirty, and at the end of the day, when I just wanted to get out of there, I'd have to clean them with, of course, more 901. I opened the doors wide, and each time the wind swung one of them closed, I sighed a bit, got up, and reopened it.

Richard came down late in the afternoon to get some tools from his truck.

"Getting it done?" he asked, as he walked past me.

I nodded. "I'm gonna finish it today." I was focused. If I kept going until it was done, I could go home and plan that stag, and I wouldn't have to worry about coming back the next day. I just had to finish the small patch of floor in the front entranceway. No more than twelve square feet.

After Richard came back in and went upstairs, I worked toward the open door, carefully soaking the floor with the 901 as far as I could. So far, I'd dumped four full containers on the ground, and had a couple of full ones left. I took a few last breaths of fresh air; I couldn't remove the last few sheets of lino without shutting the door.

As I swung that front door shut, I heard the garage door shut behind me in the laundry room. I turned and looked at it. *Whatever,* I thought. In fifteen minutes, I'd be out of there.

"Done upstairs."

I looked up to see Richard, tool box in hand.

"I've still got a bit to go," I said.

"One more job for me."

"Well, take care," I told him. "And watch out here. It's slippery." When the solvent was still active on the ground, before it evaporated into a cloud of vapour, the floor was always extremely slippery, and then became extremely sticky.

He made his way over the chemical-soaked lino backing, and I moved my body sideways so he could get past me.

"See you," he said. When he opened the door, it struck me that it was getting cool outside. He shut the door behind him.

I rearranged myself to remove those last few square feet. A whistling sound louder than anything I had ever heard, like a multitude of teakettles, filled the house. Before I had a chance to wonder about it—*BANG!*—my ears were ringing with the loudest explosion I'd ever heard, the temperature was searing, and I was surrounded by flames. Before my eyes clenched shut, stinging from the smoke, I caught a glimpse of flames dancing around me hypnotically. Just like the campfires I used to tend, only now, instead of feeling the radiant heat from a fire, I was engulfed and becoming a source of heat myself. I stood, groped for the doorknob, and pulled. I pulled with more strength than I'd ever exerted—and I was used to carrying hundreds of pounds of tools and materials on my shoulders—but that door did not open. I know now that the doors were sealed shut because the fire had created a vacuum, pulling air in from outside through any little crevice it could. I was fighting against the pressure difference inside and outside the house.

I turned and ran blindly down the hallway and into the laundry room. The fire howled. All I could hear was howling. It shrieked into my ears and my nose and pores. There was no air. I couldn't open my eyes. I could smell my clothes burning. I felt around for the handles on the door to the garage, and I pulled. Nothing. My hair was burning, each strand sizzling and stinking. My face felt strange and wrong, the skin tightening around my bones like stiff, shrinking fabric. I raced back past the half bathroom to the front door and grabbed the scorching hot knob. Adrenalin coursing through me, I pulled. I pulled and pulled. *Open, open, open,* I pleaded. But it didn't budge.

I knew I was burning, but it was unlike any burn I'd experienced, nothing like touching a hot surface or spilling hot coffee on my lap. The word *hot* comes nowhere close to what it felt like inside that house. This heat was penetrating. Later, I learned that the chemical fire reached 1500 degrees. That's double the temperature of a normal house fire. That's the temperature they use to cremate bodies. With that kind of heat, the nervous system shuts down. I wouldn't remember any pain, but I would remember torment. I would remember my skin bubbling and shrinking and tightening, and I would remember the sound of scorching hair and fabric. The life was being sapped from me, my strength was gone, and I was in sheer hell. I knew I was trapped. I knew I was going to die. But acting on instinct, I turned and ran back to the laundry room, grasped the screaming hot garage door handles, and strained against them with everything I had left. And that door still did not open.

When I let go of those door handles, I let go of the will to live. I could not bear another moment in this living hell. I was naked, tormented, and bald, and my energy was gone. My usual determination vanished. I was on fire. I collapsed into a ball, interlocked my fingers over the back of my head, tucked my face to the ground, and waited. I prayed for the last moments of my life to pass. If God had mercy, they would pass quickly.

I'd been in the fire for no more than twenty seconds when I gave up. The torment slipped away. Even though I had become kindling in a fire, I felt no pain. The howl of the inferno faded, and time slowed down. Everything was peaceful, more peaceful than anything I'd ever known. All my life, I'd been afraid of death, scared of the prospect of eternal life, which the Bible promises, but now I knew the secret: death is profound and overwhelming peace. Eternal life could only be better. I was suspended in those few sweet moments between wakefulness and sleep, when the subconscious and conscious minds collide. It was complete and perfect release. I was sinking into a sublime and eternal sleep.

I thought of Tina. And then I thought of how I'd screwed up. Reality came rushing back to me, and reality was Seba, my future child. Reality was everything I was going to miss. I'd let Tina down, and now I was letting her and our child down for the rest of their lives, burdening them with a husband and father who died at twenty-nine in an industrial fire. Who died because some stranger preferred beige linoleum to blue. Who died because he'd been too proud to phone in sick, too lazy to walk ten feet to open a laundry-room door, and too cheap to put his hammer on a sticky floor. Thoughts of the two people I loved more than myself shattered my peaceful moment. I had to try. I heard the roar of the fire again, I felt the heat penetrating even deeper, and I knew what I had to do. I had to die fighting. Fighting for what really mattered. My family.

I stood and grabbed the screaming red-hot garage door handles. They were so hot I had to force through my deepest instincts to hold them—it was like pressing my hands against a hot stove. I squeezed even tighter. I pulled one last time. The door opened.

I leapt into the garage and fell several feet into the pile of construction garbage that had been collecting for days. The lino I had just removed was on top of the pile, and it burst into flames around me. I stumbled, fighting through the rubble and fire to regain my balance, and ran toward the sunshine, toward freedom, toward safety, right through the garage and outside. Two-thirds of the way down the driveway, I collapsed into the dirt that was to become the driveway. A man threw a jug of water over my chest and then turned his garden hose on me.

Everyone was talking at once, a million voices, panicking.

"I phoned 911!"

"Who is he?"

"Oh my God!"

"Who is he?"

"Turn off the hose," someone yelled.

"Leave it on," someone else argued.

With everyone debating whether the man should continue to spray me down, he turned off the water.

"Turn it on," I begged him. "Please!" Every inch of me was crying out for the relief of that cold water, but at the urge of the crowd, he kept the hose off. I learned later that he should have left it on. A chemical burn is known as a "dirty burn" because it contaminates the body and can lead to systemic poisoning. I had already lost the protection of my skin, and was covered in solvent, glue, and melted clothes, along with whatever else had stuck to me in the garage. The water wouldn't have endangered me any more than the chemical was already doing, and would at least have cooled me down. My body was so hot, I was still burning as I lay there.

"I'm a nurse," said a woman crouched by my head. She told me an ambulance was on its way. "What's your name?" she asked. "Are you married? Where's your wife? What's her cell number?"

I gave her the number. "Tina's pregnant," I said. I couldn't get this thought out of my head. "My wife's pregnant."

Once I knew Tina was on her way to the hospital, I let go and panicked. "What's wrong with my lips?" I screamed. "What's wrong with my lips?" I could smell charred flesh—my flesh—but all I could feel were my lips, swelling and burning like they'd been stung by a million bees.

The nurse was talking, asking me more questions, but I couldn't focus on what she was saying. An ambulance siren wailed, off in the distance.

"Is my penis gone?" I asked. My groin was starting to hurt as much as my lips, but I still couldn't feel anything else. I was too afraid to look at myself. "Are my fingers gone? My ears? My toes?"

"They're all there," the nurse kept reassuring me. She must have known some of them wouldn't be there for long. Luckily for my groin, it hurt the most because my work belt had protected it. It was slightly burned, but not badly enough to cause the nerve damage that left the majority of my body numb.

"Where's the ambulance?" I asked.

"It's coming, Spencer."

The sirens wailed and wailed, closer and closer but not close enough.

"How am I going to support my family?" I screamed. "My life is over." Once this thought was in my head, I screamed it again and again. "My life is over! My life is over. I'm going to die. Please God, take me." Sometimes at night, I wonder how much it affected those onlookers to see that naked, bald, and extremely burned man screaming at the top of his lungs that his life was over.

The sirens came closer.

The nurse kept talking to me, trying to calm me down, but I couldn't stop screaming. Where was the ambulance? I could hear it, but it was taking forever. They were actually following the smoke, but couldn't find the entrance to the cul de sac; luckily, a bystander drove over and showed them how to get to me.

The sirens came closer.

"Let them through!" shouted the nurse.

A paramedic kneeled in front of me. He leaned over, his eyes a foot from my own, and we stared at each other. Although I wouldn't remember what he looked like, whether he was young or old or handsome—I wouldn't even be completely sure if it had been a man or a woman—that paramedic's expression of sheer panic was burned permanently into my memory. That was the moment I knew just how badly I was hurt, and I'll never forget the horror I saw in those eyes. He quickly tried to regain his composure, but I had already seen through it. I knew what he knew. He was looking into the face of death. I was a goner.

• • •

In the Belly of a Whale

The Edmonton Eskimos would play Montreal that November for the Grey Cup, in Regina, and Marc and I had bought tickets before the fire. But in my dream, we were driving into Winnipeg, and it was winter, and snowing, and so cold the streets were deserted, the snowbanks up to my waist.

"I'll just pick up my uncle," Marc said, turning into an alley behind a row of ramshackle bungalows. He pulled into the driveway behind one house that looked sixty or seventy years old and badly maintained, and we hurried through the cutting cold, in the back door, and down a flight of stairs.

"This is my uncle," Marc said. "Don Cherry." It was Don Cherry, all right—Canada's infamous hockey commentator sitting right there on a decrepit old sofa. Marc and I waited while Don chatted, taking his sweet time with his winter gear. I wished Marc would tell his uncle to stop talking and hurry up. Sure enough, by the time we went back outside, the car was hopelessly stuck, buried in snow halfway up its tires.

"Great!" I said. "Do you have any idea how long I've been waiting to go to this game?"

"Never mind," said Don Cherry. "We'll walk. It's not far."

As we started down the alley, the freezing wind and snow stung me all over. Why didn't I have a warm coat and a thick toque like Marc and his uncle did? I didn't even have gloves, and it was too late to go back and get them. Even as we approached the stadium and found ourselves in the midst of a boisterous crowd, the cold penetrated my thin jacket. I was desperate to get inside.

But Marc and Don Cherry were gone. I couldn't see them anywhere.

"Marc," I yelled. "You have my ticket. Where are you, man?"

I watched in disappointment and mounting desperation as the whole eager crowd disappeared into the heated stadium. As the last of them went in, the doors closed, and the sound of laughter and cheering was replaced by silence. My friends had gone on without me; the doors were locked. I was alone and freezing in an unfamiliar place, all my plans thwarted.

Then a lone figure came toward me through the snow. An Aboriginal man. He saw I was in trouble. He knew I needed to find warmth, and I knew he would help me.

Come, he motioned, as he grabbed me by the arm.

I followed him to the river and we both dove under the water. When I opened my eyes, I saw a huge whale suspended under the water and held by ropes to the river bottom. It was dead. We swam closer, then dove straight down, and when we swam under the whale I noticed a large cut in its belly. The man guided me inside. In the belly of that whale, my friend made a fire. He protected me, and made sure I was warm. I knew I was safe.

• • •

For my first six weeks at the University of Alberta Hospital's Firefighters' Burn Treatment Unit, I was in a medically induced coma, which isn't really a coma at all. I was not technically unconscious, but was heavily sedated and sometimes on muscle relaxants that paralyzed my body. The doctors who treated me explained later that I could hear and even respond to voices, but the drugs they gave me induced amnesia. That's why, for most patients, a medically induced coma leaves a complete blank in their memory. The burn unit staff kept me in this state because I underwent surgery almost every other day, and my body was going through so much trauma, it was best if I didn't experience or remember it at all.

I don't remember that time in a normal way, but I do remember the most vivid dreams of my life. A year later, my psychologist would tell me I wasn't the type to repress traumatic memories or turn away from difficult truths. I believe that while my ability to understand and remember was suppressed, my brain used dreams to process what was going on around me. I never dreamed that I was burned because I wasn't ready to face it, but my mind was so determined to grasp the reality of those first six weeks, it used dreams to gradually give me as much of the truth as I could bear.

Pastor Habben visited me even when I was in that sedated state, and I learned later that he read to me from the scriptures, specifically Exodus 14. As Moses leads the Israelites out of slavery, he finds himself surrounded by Egyptians on three sides and sea on the fourth. The Israelites despair—surely it would have been better to remain in slavery than to die—but Moses assures them there is nothing to fear. "The Lord will fight for you," Moses tells his people as the army closes in on them, "and you have only to keep still."

Pastor Habben said, "Spencer, you're a *go-go-go* person; you're an *I'm-gonna-fix-it* person. You can't fix it. But you know what? You have the Lord who is fighting for you. You only need to be still."

I think my dreams gave me a chance to do that, huddled inside my own mind as in the belly of a whale. I had dreams that reworked my trauma as I wished it had happened: in one recurring sequence, I led a firefighting team through a raging forest fire, and I led us to victory against those flames. My team and I were always equipped with blanket-sized pieces of leather that were called "bear huggers." When I saw a blast of flames getting too close, I yelled, "Drop to the ground! Cover yourselves!" I pulled the heavy, leather blanket over me, and seconds later I heard the fire roaring over and around me. I wasn't afraid; I was safe, and I knew all my men were safe, too. I would eventually learn that the term "bear hugger" had entered my mind through the haze of drugs. It actually referred to a heavy blanket used for patients who couldn't control their body temperatures. Burn patients, like me.

Some dreams fit clearly with my physical state and my treatment. I often found myself in wintry places. Sometimes I was skiing, and sometimes I was huddled helplessly in a plane that had crashed into a frozen lake. Either way, as my body temperature fluctuated in that hospital bed, I dreamed of cold. I often dreamed a stranger was fitting me with new clothes. After wrapping the fabric around my body, he stuck countless steel pins through the fabric and into my skin. I wanted to run, but couldn't move. I was helpless, weak, and terrified. I learned later that Dr. P. and the other surgeons had removed all the burnt tissue from my body and stapled cadaver skin in its place. They replaced that cadaver skin often, and I believe that's why this dream was the only one that reoccurred.

In one horrifying dream, my penis was cut off. That wasn't entirely inaccurate: the surgeons circumcised me and used the foreskin to replace my eyelids. "And we replaced the skin under your eyes with grafts from your scrotum," Dr. P. would tell me. "Don't worry. There's plenty left." Well, that explained why I had curly little hairs growing out of my face!

"Guess what," I told my brothers after I learned the origin of my eyelids. "I'm a dickhead."

"We already knew that," Craig said.

"I'm cockeyed," I said. "I have great foresight!"

To this day, Reagan thinks my new eyelids are hilarious. He likes to tell people I get an erection if I blink quickly. Strangely, my brothers were both circumcised, but when I was born, my parents decided to forego the procedure. Someone up there must have whispered in their ears, *He's going to need that skin.*

There were also Aboriginal people in many of my dreams, and they usually played a nurturing, understanding role. Again and again, these Native figures saved my life with their compassion. Tina's family is Métis, and her grandmother is a status Indian, though you would never guess it, looking at Tina. As my mind struggled to understand what had happened to me, Tina's presence in my hospital room, and sometimes the presence of her mother and stepfather, Deb and Ken, as well, gave me comfort and the will to live.

Other dreams were less obvious in their symbolism, and some I don't understand to this day. The city of Winnipeg took on a special significance for me, and many of the dreams were set there. I don't know why that was, since I'd never been there. I may have focused on Winnipeg, also known as "Winterpeg," because I couldn't stay warm, and it's one of the coldest cities in the world.

I had my most frightening dreams as the doctors slowly brought me out of the induced coma. I was asleep and deep in dreamland all night, and during the days I was awake but hallucinating and not quite all there. The dreams I had between dreamland and consciousness were the worst. They were all variations on a theme, though the scenarios were different. Sometimes I would be in a Second World War fighter or in a bike race or even in ancient Egypt, but as the dream ended I always found myself trapped. Nothing happened. I survived whatever the dream was about, but then sat there, unable to move or to call for help, as nobody was there to hear me. Anxiety set in and panic overtook me; it was extremely frightening to be trapped in a dream that had ended. Fear ripped through me.

Then a nurse came into my room to administer more drugs or check my vitals, and freed me from that state. In my dreams, I learned to control the anxiety by saying to myself, "Relax, Spencer. Somebody always comes in and saves you. Be patient." It was a horrible feeling to be caught in that dream state. I felt like I was frozen in time.

• • •

As I gradually came out of the coma, I was still in a fog of drugs. The doctors had me on Ativan for anxiety, plus antidepressants and an assortment of painkillers. I was on insulin because I'd developed a form of temporary, burn-induced diabetes. I became addicted to Ativan, morphine, methadone, and Tylenol 3, but at the time, they saved me. I felt no pain, except when I slid down the bed, which happened constantly, leaving my feet pushed helplessly against the footboard. The pressure of my body weight against the soles of my feet, which had already been used for countless skin grafts, had me reeling in pain.

All the antidepressants in the world couldn't have numbed me to the misery of my situation. I was in isolation because the greatest danger to burn patients comes from bacteria, often from bacteria that are picked up in the burn unit. With so many open wounds, infections quickly become deadly. A list on my door, approved by Tina, specified the few people allowed to visit me, and each person who entered my room scrubbed up and gowned up so only their eyes showed. It would be a long time before I saw hair again, or street clothes. I never learned to recognize the medical teams' faces under their yellow masks, even those of the people I saw every day: my occupational therapist, Diana, my physical therapist, Sharon, and my nurse, a man named Rudi.

There were many others who came and went. Only one person was in my room for hours every day, and that was Tina. My mother came regularly as well, and Pastor Habben brought prayers and devotions. Sometimes Tina's mother and stepfather visited, but they were mostly busy helping Tina with everything else. My brothers took some months to gather their courage after the trauma of seeing me the day I was burned, and my father never came to see me until he knew I was there, as the Spencer he remembered. It took many months for that Spencer to start to surface through the haze of drugs, pain, and anger, but when I started coming out of my depression, my father was a regular visitor, and he, I could recognize under the mask.

All around me, and through me, were machines. The 901 fumes had ignited inside my lungs, and those burns meant I needed a ventilator. The tube was wired to my teeth and inserted down my throat, which meant I couldn't speak. Tubes stuck out from each side of my chest, draining fluid from my damaged lungs. My left lung eventually collapsed, that side of my diaphragm permanently paralyzed.

I soon realized my hands were damaged beyond repair. My fingers had all been amputated at the first or second joints, my left pinky removed completely. "There's a pin through each of your fingers to prevent your hands from curling into useless fists," Sharon explained. It was hard to imagine those hands more useless than they already were. The pins were soon removed, and then Diana and Sharon both came every day to stretch the remnants of my fingers and splint them. They told me they were working to keep my joints and muscles flexible.

Ninety percent of my body was covered in cadaver skin or Integra, a new technology that acts as skin. Blood vessels grow into it, and it forms a base for skin grafts. Dr. P. and the other surgeons gradually replaced the cadaver skin with grafts made from my own unburned skin. Every six weeks the cadaver skin was replaced before my body rejected it.

I couldn't swallow food, so I had a feeding tube through my nose. Eventually, it was surgically inserted through my abdomen into my stomach. The hospital's dietician, Kara, explained they'd started me on a nasal-gastric feeding tube within hours of being admitted. "We're feeding you constantly," she said, "and we're giving you 3700 calories per day. That might sound like a lot, but after a burn like yours, the body's metabolic rate doubles, and you need twice the calories." She explained that while my metabolism skyrocketed, another process called "catabolism" kicked in. When a patient is badly burned, his body is so desperate for energy it starts to break down its own muscle tissue for fuel. "It's impossible to stop that process," Kara said, "but we can slow it down a bit with a high protein diet."

The worst thing was, I couldn't move. I couldn't roll over. I couldn't sit up. I couldn't lift my legs or arms, or even wiggle my toes. When Sharon came to stretch my limbs each day, she started by asking me to lift my arms and legs myself. I couldn't. She had to move each limb for me. I was weak because of muscle loss; when Dr. P. told me I had third and fourth degree burns, he meant the burns had penetrated my skin, through the fatty tissue under the skin and into the muscle. That burned tissue was dead, and had to be removed surgically.

I lost more muscle to the catabolic reaction Kara had warned me about, and still more to atrophy. I lost 33 percent of my body weight, leaving me, at my most emaciated, at 112 pounds. Not exactly my idea of manly. Pastor Habben had advised me to be still; I didn't have much choice. My only option was to trust that God was fighting for me, and I tried to focus on that trust. That trust was the only thing between me and despair. Some days I believed that God knew best, but other days I asked Him, "Why me?" Sometimes I blamed Him. It was a constant battle of faith and hope and anger, and I couldn't control any of them.

With nothing else to do, I spent my waking hours replaying the fire in my head. No one knew I remembered the accident, and they seemed to assume I didn't. I couldn't speak because of the ventilator in my mouth, so I was in my own private hell in more ways than one. Since I couldn't move my hands it was almost impossible to communicate, and the only emotion I could, and did, convey was frustration; I did this by rolling my eyes. I still didn't have enough skin on my eyelids to blink properly—that would take several surgeries—so I also had to roll my eyes back to moisten them. Anyone watching would have thought I was frustrated every ten seconds. And they probably would have been right.

My next-door neighbour, who happened to be an occupational therapist, heard about my problems communicating. She suggested a board with each letter of the alphabet and a series of pictures across the bottom. My mother tried it out, moving one finger slowly through the alphabet.

"Just nod when she gets to the right letter," Tina told me.

I waited until Mom reached the *i,* and then nodded. Then I waited until she reached the *m,* but by the time I managed to move my head, her finger had moved on.

"*In*?" said my mother.

I rolled my eyes.

"Not *in*? Should I keep going?"

I had no way to tell her we'd miscommunicated. I stared up at the ceiling.

It was too frustrating. I was exhausted.

"Did I get a letter wrong?" she asked.

I nodded.

"The *i?*"

I rolled my eyes.

"The *n?*"

I nodded.

She began again at *a*. Finally, after what seemed like an exhausting hour, I managed to spell out the simple message, "I'm cold."

As Diana placed another blanket over me, taking care to cover my feet, which always seemed to stick out the bottom despite everyone's best efforts, Tina suggested, "Just spell *cold,* Spence. We'll know what you mean."

For some reason even I don't understand, I persisted in spelling only complete sentences on that board. Those sentences were short, and they were usually "Change the channel," "I'm cold," or "Please read." I didn't have a lot else to say. I was bored. Nothing happened, nothing changed. I had surgeries and more surgeries. As one part of my body started to heal, another was bandaged. I was wrapped almost head-to-foot in gauze except during bandage changes. Despite the therapists' daily routines, I seemed to be getting worse. When I caught a glimpse of my unbandaged legs, they looked like sticks. Over those bony limbs, the skin was a patchwork of grafts with red in between as though my stuffing were coming out. It was hard to believe those legs were mine.

If Tina hadn't told me the date every morning when she came in, I could easily have lost track of the days or even months. When she told me it was June 20, she added, "Remember, you have surgery scheduled tomorrow." An upcoming surgery was always great news. I looked forward to surgery more than anything else, second only to having my bandages changed. Each time I received a new skin graft, I met with my favourite person in the hospital:

the anaesthesiologist. When the mask came over my face, I knew I was in for a few blessed hours of rest. No memories, no dreams, no torment. Some surgery required full thickness grafts. Bolis bandages were stitched on over the graft to apply pressure and aid in attaching a blood supply to the new skin. After a week, the nurses dosed me with ketamine, a short-term general anaesthetic, to remove the bandages. I thought of my hours in surgery and on ketamine as free time, time that passed without me having to experience it.

As I luxuriated in the prospect of my upcoming surgery, Tina added, "It's our anniversary, our fifth wedding anniversary, next week." I nodded as vigorously as I could to let her know I hadn't forgotten that date.

Until I fell into my drug-induced sleep that night, I thought about my upcoming anniversary. When I married Tina, I'd vowed to stand by her side, to provide for our family, to be strong. Now I couldn't do any of those things. Instead I lay helpless and possibly dying as she carried our child. I had to at least give her an anniversary present. At least a card. There had to be a way.

I was also nervous about the next day. I had the bliss of anaesthesia to look forward to, but I was anxious; I always dreaded the hour before surgery. Each time, a team of nurses prepared me for the trip through the hospital, and since they couldn't bring all the hefty machinery that kept me alive, they disconnected my ventilator and used a manual hand pump to give me air en route to the OR. This was terrifying, because as soon as they disconnected that mechanical ventilator, I couldn't breathe. I don't understand it fully, but I would try to breathe; I would expand my chest and flex my diaphragm, but nothing would happen. As the nurses wheeled me down the hall, one kept a hand on the bag now secured over my face, and each time she squeezed it, I received a breath of air. The nurse, occupied with five or six other matters along with the small concern of my lungs, often seemed to miss a breath, or at least wait longer than was comfortable. I couldn't speak or move—I could only struggle in vain to fill my lungs, with no way of giving a sign. The nurse always delivered the next breath before I suffocated, but I was panicky all the way to the OR. There, they immediately hooked me back up to a mechanical ventilator. After that, it was only seconds until I heard the words I longed for: "Okay, let's put him under."

• • •

The morning of the surgery, my mother visited me for a few hours. I was happy to see her, partly because I wanted her to buy an anniversary card for Tina. I wanted to explain what she should write for me, to express my love and gratitude for Tina's unwavering support. But it wasn't working. My mother knew I wanted to tell her something, and she kept reciting the alphabet, but when the nurses came to get me, I'd only communicated the letter *a*. The nurses detached me from the machine and transferred me to a stretcher, and my mother kept slowly going through the alphabet, waiting for me to nod. I spelled out two *n*'s, and as they wheeled me out of the room, my mother followed, still trying to figure out what I wanted so badly to communicate.

Just as the elevator door opened, Mom got it. "An anniversary card for Tina!" A wave of relief flooded over me. I nodded. "Don't worry, honey," Mom called after me as I felt the bump of the stretcher entering the elevator. "I'll make sure I do that for you." I knew she'd pick out the right card and sign it on my behalf. I was so relieved I barely noticed I wasn't panicking over my breathing.

After that skin graft, on the morning of our fifth wedding anniversary, my nurse Rudi had another surprise for me. Really, it was a surprise for everyone, since no one knew what was to happen that day except Dr. P. and the burn unit nurses. "You're ready to breathe by yourself," Rudi said. "Happy anniversary."

Dr. P. came to my room with a respiration specialist. I was excited to lose the ventilator, and also scared that it would be painful—and, of course, that I wouldn't be able to breathe. But they pulled it, and it seemed like nothing. It didn't hurt, and I was breathing on my own. They asked me to cough, and I tried. "Can you speak?" asked Dr. P. He was concerned that my vocal cords might have been stretched and damaged by the ventilator.

"What do you want me to say," I managed raspingly, in my usual sarcastic manner.

These were the first things I'd done on my own since the fire: breathing and talking. Now I could put away the communication board and communicate normally. That day was the first, after the fire, that I can actually remember being happy.

I waited eagerly for Tina, and when she arrived on the burn unit, no one told her the ventilator was out; the nurses just told her something good had happened. I heard her in the little prep room, washing her hands and fumbling with her sterile clothes. I was so excited I couldn't wait any longer. It had been a long day for me, waiting to talk to her with my own words, rather than by nodding at a board or rolling my eyes in frustration. I couldn't wait to tell her how much I loved her. It meant so much to me to express that sentiment, especially since I'd failed to say it in the Emergency Room the day of my fire.

When she finally was all washed and gowned up, which seemed to take forever, she opened the door and I let out the loudest whisper I could muster.

"I love you."

That was her fifth wedding anniversary gift, and I don't think I'll ever be able to top it.

• • •

The Waters Closed In

Speaking had always been my favourite activity, but now that I could do it again, I found I didn't have much to say. My insights were reduced to how tired I was, or that my feet hurt; and my concerns were reduced to questions like: "Can I get a popsicle?" "Can I have some apple juice?" and "Where's Tina?" I couldn't pronounce certain letters properly, and people had to lean close to my face to hear me. I hated having to repeat myself, and I didn't have anything important to share anyway, because my life didn't change. I'd been excited to express myself again, but the sentiments I had to express were not pleasant. I was miserable.

In my nightmares, I was stuck, and when I was awake, my life was stuck at the moment of the fire, like a scratched CD playing the same riff again and again, unable to move forward. My tormenting, repetitive memories and the monotony of my life dragged me down, and all I wanted was to sleep. I was tired enough to dream my days away, but fortunately or unfortunately, I was never allowed to sleep in past seven. The mornings were always busy with therapy and bandage changes, and I had another therapy session after lunch. Then I stewed in my room, watching TV until someone decided to visit me.

I didn't get a lot of visitors other than Tina, who was there every day. My mother came fairly often, along with Tina's mother and stepfather and sometimes Pastor Habben or someone from the congregation. I kept the list short. I could have had more visitors, and Tina was always telling me about people who wanted to see me, but I didn't want them looking at me, and I didn't want their company or their sympathy. I didn't want to be reminded that time hadn't stopped in the real world. The race continued without me; my friends' lives continued and changed and grew. Everyone changed around me, and I remained the same. Trapped in a body that had once felt capable of anything.

That's when I experienced first-hand how depression chases away the people you love. The only people I truly wanted to see were Tina, my mother, and sometimes Pastor Habben; when they were there, I felt better—as content as I was capable of feeling. I deeply regret that I never told them so at the time, but I was too depressed to express any positive emotions, including gratitude or love. It may seem obvious that someone in my situation would sink into despair and apathy, and the doctors had anticipated it, which was why my bloodstream was thick with antidepressants. As time went by, I didn't have the strength to hope for anything or care about anyone. I replayed memories from my former life, compared them with my days in the hospital, and realized with ever-increasing poignancy what I'd lost. I was sure I would never get my former life—my former self—back. I realize now that I convinced myself of things that weren't true.

I still had a feeding tube that delivered calories into my stomach twenty-four hours a day, though I could now chew and swallow pureed food. I couldn't move my arms, so I couldn't feed myself. I was on so many pills I drank a litre of apple juice each morning to wash them down. My lungs had still not entirely healed, and every day for months I discharged large quantities of phlegm.

And then there was the daily humiliation of what the medical professionals called "toileting." A catheter allowed me to urinate, and to control when I urinated, but I dreaded bowel movements because the drugs affected my bowel control, and my backside was a patchwork of partly healed skin grafts, so I couldn't bear contact with the steel bedpan. The nurses had to change my sheets and clean me up at least once a day. It would be nine months after the accident when I finally claimed the decency of using a bedpan.

Sharon always talked to me as she went through her physical therapy routine, chatting about current events or telling me about all the things I'd be able to do again. She said I'd move back home, that I'd walk, that I'd work in my garden again, and do all the things I loved. I learned much later that Sharon asked Tina, "Spencer's a quiet guy, isn't he? Was he always so subdued? Is he shy?"

Tina laughed. "You don't know Spencer!" she said.

If Sharon had known me better, she might have realized how depressed I was, how unlike my former self. I watched her work on my useless body and I didn't believe a word she said. I knew I was never getting out of that bed. My life was gone. I was useless. How could I ever be a husband again, or become a father? How could I be a man?

Four days after I regained my voice, I told Tina, "I'm not the man you married. Leave me. Take everything and go; I'll understand."

"Shut up, Spencer," Tina said. Her belly was so round now that she didn't stand up to make her point. "That the stupidest thing I ever heard you say."

"What use am I to you?"

"You stupid man," Tina sighed. "Never say that again."

"I love it when you call me stupid," I said.

"You're an idiot!"

"Sweetest thing you ever said."

Tina used a tissue to blot a tear from my cheek. I hadn't even realized I was crying. Or maybe I wasn't—my eyes were always watering. Of course I didn't want Tina to leave me. But what could I do? What could I offer?

"I can't wait to make love to you again," I rasped.

Tina laughed. "Trust you to still be thinking about that right now!"

"Can I touch you?"

Tina stood beside the bed and lifted my arm to place my hand on her belly. "The baby's kicking," she said. I couldn't feel a thing.

"Can I touch your face?" I asked.

Tina moved my hand.

• • •

Tina did her best to keep me updated on the outside world, and to keep me entertained. Unfortunately, her life began to slow down along with mine, her days spent between my room, the nurses' station, and the hospital cafeteria. She found time for her own medical checkups, which were important since she was in the last trimester of her pregnancy.

Tina kept a notebook of events and news, and things that had happened while I was sedated, and the contents of Tina's notebook gave me new things to think about, just as it reminded me how quickly the world was going on without me.

One of Tina's biggest pieces of news was that Marc had a wonderful new girlfriend.

Janice, I thought.

"Her name's Janice," Tina said. "They seem pretty serious."

Somehow I'd known Janice's name before Tina said it. I must have heard it while I was comatose, along with the term "bear hugger," and filed it away.

Tina often read to me from a book of devotions from my church; she knew they would give me comfort and food for thought even though she wasn't religious herself. When she wasn't reading devotions, Tina picked up the book I'd started before the fire, *The Fellowship of the Ring*, the first in the *Lord of Rings* trilogy. I could have immersed myself in that world for hours, but I knew it wasn't interesting for Tina, who had trouble keeping track of all the characters and struggled with their names. I knew she was extremely bored, but she read to me anyway. Usually I absorbed only a few passages before letting her off the hook. I didn't want to torture her for too long. Often, she brought in movies, and we watched them together. We watched the *Lord of the Rings* trilogy, and my favourite movie of all time, *Braveheart*. That movie has it all: love, betrayal, war, bloodshed, humour, and a good storyline.

Sadly, I spent the vast majority of my time watching television. Countless hours of shows and movies provided the only respite from thinking and remembering. What else could I do? I realized something surprising. My tastes had changed. TV shows that had once seemed funny had lost all their humour. I'm talking about shows like *America's Funniest Home Videos* and *Don Cherry's Rock 'em Sock 'em Hockey*. Shows about people getting hurt. Sure, it looked funny when someone was hit with a softball or bitten by a dog, or when a hockey player got checked so hard he did flips on the ice. But what those videos didn't show was the pain. I used to laugh at those shows, but now I found I could only think of the time afterward. The time that person spent in the hospital, painfully rebuilding his body and his life.

If Richard, the witness to my accident, had filmed a home movie that day, it would show a solid wall of flames through the front window of a new house. It would show that wall of flames move sideways, and you would realize you were looking at limbs—a figure—moving through the inferno. I doubt anyone would be tempted to laugh as a six foot three, naked, bald, burning man fell five feet into a pile of garbage, and it would not seem so funny when that garbage exploded into flames, the man struggled to his feet, ran up the unfinished driveway, and rolled in the dirt. If the camera zoomed in on my face, you might think I was strangely calm, giving instructions and reciting Tina's cellphone number, and then you would see me start to panic, screaming that my life was over. You would see me ask again and again if my nose was still there, and my ears and my fingers and my penis. You would see the last moments I ever looked anything close to normal, and certainly the last moments I ever felt normal.

I'd always had a partially photographic memory. I vividly remembered moments from my early childhood; I remembered my abusive daycare attendant; I remembered spotting bottles on the side of the road and yelling at my parents to stop so Craig could collect them, and later cash them in to buy our own tickets to Hawaii. I remembered my first kiss and I remembered each panicky moment of the car accident I was in when I was sixteen. I remembered phone numbers and birthdays and even small things, like the jeans and tee-shirt Tina wore when we packed up our first apartment and escaped in the middle of the night, turning only to say good riddance to a leaky bedroom ceiling and an unpaid landlord.

And I didn't regret remembering the fire in such perfect detail. It would have been far worse to lie there wondering what had happened. The bad part was replaying it again and again right up to the moment when the paramedic leaned over me. I couldn't get his expression out of my head: that look of horror, as though he saw the whole wretched path ahead of me written on my skin. Lying in that bed, day after day after day, I obsessed over what I could have done differently. I thought about all the people who'd wronged me.

Soon every moment, every waking thought, was anger that this had to happen.

I blamed God. *Why me?* I demanded. *What have I done to deserve this?*

I thought of all the people who'd failed to speak out and question our lino-stripping method, whose carelessness, ineptitude, and cowardice had put me in that bed, immobile and emaciated. I couldn't understand Richard, who left the house moments before the fire. Why hadn't he turned back and opened the door? Why hadn't he helped me? I blamed the homebuilders and the supplier that sent the wrong lino; I even wanted to sue them, but no lawyer would touch the case. I blamed the homeowners, who in my mind had cared more about the colour of their lino than my safety. I blamed the inventor of Roberts 1901. I blamed my parents for steering me toward floor laying when they should have seen I was smart enough to be a lawyer or an accountant—the kind of professional that doesn't get blown up on the job. I blamed everyone I could think of. I even blamed the doctors, therapists, and nurses for causing me discomfort every day, for not making me better faster, or simply for not coming fast enough when I called. And, of course,

I blamed Jack. How could he have let me use that chemical when he knew how dangerous it was? His licence plate: K-BOOM. It was so sick, now. And we'd all laughed about Jack's business partner running down the street in his socks. *Try running down the street naked,* I thought. *Naked and on fire, with your skin sloughing off.*

Before I could talk, I'd had a constant stream of Ativan, antidepressants, and painkillers administered through my feeding tube. They kept my anxiety under control. But after the ventilator was pulled, I started taking my drugs orally. I was more and more responsible for controlling my pain and my anxiety, and I had to ask for the drugs. I had to wait a certain number of hours between each dose, but I couldn't turn my head to see the clock hanging on the wall over my head. Then I noticed that at 12:05, the clock always clicked. That sound, just after noon and midnight, was my only measure of time passing, and I used it to estimate when I could get my next dose of drugs. Still, without the constant stream of Ativan I'd become used to, my despair gave way to what I can only call two weeks of full-blown insanity.

Every evening, starting around five o'clock, I had a strange sensation of dread. Slowly, it became worse and worse. My breath became shallow and fast, and my heart raced. Sometimes I was delusional. One day I believed I was in the sewers of New York, fighting alligators; Rudi realized I had watched *Men in Black* earlier that day, and I couldn't distinguish the movie, with its aliens in New York City, from real life. Sometimes I was scared for no reason at all. I couldn't operate the call bell the nurses had given me, which made me feel even more helpless and desperate. That's when the panic overtook me.

I screamed at the top of my lungs, and I learned to scream pretty loudly. The nurses let me holler for a while, and finally they came in. They didn't understand why I was screaming, and I don't think they ever could. In all my time on the burn unit, I never heard another patient scream the way I did. I wanted someone in the room, but if a nurse came, I often just wanted to be alone again. The people whose presence I could tolerate were Tina and my mom. Once I was screaming so loudly, and my breathing was so uncontrollable, that one of my nurses came in and sat with me to watch hockey. Well, that backfired. He provided a loud commentary on the game until I only wanted him to leave. Of course, I am now thankful for his kindness and for giving of himself when I really needed it. He did help me that evening because when he left I was more focused on being angry with him for coming in and ruining the hockey game than I was on the panic. Usually, as each nurse walked out the door, fear of being alone with my demons began to set in again. At nine o'clock, the horror finally ended as the nurses gave me my sleeping pills.

Tina sat with me each evening for those two weeks. If it hadn't been for her courage and strength, I don't know if I would have returned to a normal presence of mind. I use the term "normal" loosely. As I regained my grip on reality, I knew I would never work again. No one would ever love me again. What did I have to offer Tina, our baby, or the world? The answer was plain: nothing. I was preoccupied with one desire: the desire to kill myself. That peace I felt when I lay on the laundry room floor, my body on fire, waiting to die. I wanted to sink back into that feeling, forever.

"I don't care. Do what it takes. I don't want to die." I remembered how certain I'd felt when I'd spoken those words. I'd always considered myself strong, but I had known nothing, when I made that choice, of what was in store for me. Of what real pain was. The words "quality of life" had been vague; the words "third and fourth degree burns" nearly meaningless. Yes, I had chosen to live, but now I thought about suicide constantly, trying to conceive of a way to do it, as though looking for the missing piece to a puzzle. I obsessed over my dilemma. I couldn't grab a knife; I didn't have the strength to lift a gun or pull the trigger, even if could get one. I didn't have the dexterity to remove the cap from a bottle of pills. The fact was, I couldn't move my arm the few feet it would take to pull the plug on my own feeding tube.

Now I'm grateful I was incapable of acting on my suicidal impulses, and I would never condone suicide for anyone. When death comes, I'll meet it with a smile, looking forward to that experience again. But not until it's my time. I know now that life is worth living, even being burnt. Even since the breakdown of my marriage. But lying in that hospital bed, my inability to kill myself made me hate my life and myself even more. Every time I came to the conclusion that I couldn't even kill myself, it reinforced how useless I really was, and that fed my anger and despair. I wanted, even more, to die. I was stuck in a vicious circle, one that ate away at my will to live and left nothing but a useless shell of a man.

• • •

I don't know what would have become of me otherwise, but on September 28, 2003, five months and four days after the fire, everything changed. I woke up to fluorescent hospital lights, and my father-in-law standing over me. "Tina's in labour," he told me.

It was three in the morning, and I slipped in and out of sleep, waking each time to Ken's pacing. The truth is, I didn't want to be awake. What use was I, lying there, waiting? This was supposed to have been the happiest day of my life, and I was in the wrong hospital, disabled and maimed, lost in a narcotic haze, missing the birth of my child, something I had dreamed of for so long, even back when I was in high school. I was so excited when Tina first told me she was pregnant. And now when my dream of family was to finally happen, I would miss it all.

We'd arranged a teleconferencing link with the hospital where Tina would give birth, but by the time she arrived there, she'd already given birth. Her labour had only lasted three and a half hours, and her mother had delivered the baby on our bed, with the instruction of a 911 operator. To this day, I can't help but feel robbed of that experience. Although I am truly grateful that Tina's mother, Deb, was there to help her and deliver our baby, to me something was gained and taken away that night. If I hadn't been burned, I would have been there for my wife when she gave birth and would have had the extreme honour of delivering our child.

Tina and I spoke briefly in the early hours that morning, by telephone, after she was settled into the hospital. The baby was healthy and Tina was doing fine; that was good to hear. I went to sleep.

• • •

Tina came the next day, and she brought our daughter. "Do you want to hold her?" she asked.

Of course I did, but I couldn't even turn my head, let alone lift my arms. Tina raised the bed's railing and padded it with a blanket, and then she lowered a little bundle into the crook of my arm. My daughter was gowned up just like everyone else; she was wrapped in a sterile pillowcase. I couldn't feel her against my skin, but I felt her life force there, and I looked at her in awe. Her sweet face with its button nose and brand-new ears, and her tiny, amazing fingers and toes. Everything I'd lost, she had.

After about two minutes of that eight pounds and six ounces, her little body weight became too much for me. I tried so hard to not let go of her. I sucked up the pain, trying to hold on for as long as I could. That was the first time I tried to fight through the pain—a pain that was soon to become all too familiar. After I couldn't stand it anymore, I swallowed my pride and some tears, and asked Tina to take our child away. I didn't say why. It hurt so much to have to ask, after such a short time, to have my baby taken out of my arms. I wanted to hold her forever.

But my daughter and I made a trade that day. I'd helped Tina give our child life, and now Tina and that child gave me the strength and conviction to keep living. This baby needed a dad, and Tina needed a husband. And I was so far from being either of those things. I had no idea how I was going to do it, but I knew I had to try. I had to stop feeling sorry for myself. I had to co-operate with the therapists. And I had to deal with the pain; I had to, eventually, get off the drugs. I had to believe I could get better. I had to get home. This was what it meant to be a parent: I could no longer be selfish. My eyes finally opened, and I realized I had the most amazing woman who needed me to fight, and a perfectly healthy little girl who needed a daddy.

Tina and I named our daughter Amber. I'd always wanted my child to have a name that went with "Beach." I'd suggested Rose, Pebble, Sandy, I even tried for Municipal—you name it; Tina said no. Amber was the one name we agreed on, and I especially liked it because amber is my Grandmother Jekabson's favourite gemstone. Tina's stepfather, Ken, joked that the name was a combination of *amb*ulance and ER, for Emergency Room.

My life and attitude did not change instantly with Amber's birth, but I did stop obsessing about death. I dared to believe I might get better, and I began to suspect I was strong enough to get through this test. I wanted more than anything to be a good father, to help my daughter face the world head-on and without fear. As I'd always said, when a person has a desire that strong, he'll do incredible things to fulfill that desire. Finally that truth was working for me instead of against me. I promised myself I would fight. I had no idea what that promise would mean.

• • •

Over the next months, I moved in fits and starts toward a new, more positive attitude. Some days I took steps forward, and some days I took a step back. My next big step forward came on Boxing Day that year, when I was finally allowed to leave the hospital and visit my house for a few hours. Of course, I had wanted to go on Christmas, but that was too hard to schedule. I needed an ambulance and paramedics to take me home and bring me back. I'd be on a stretcher the whole time, and because I was afraid I'd have to use the bathroom during my visit, two nurses would accompany me, to help if I needed it. My anticipation built for weeks, and finally Christmas came and went.

The paramedics showed up a little late, around two o'clock, and the two nurses rode in the back of the ambulance with me. My father-in-law had built a little ramp so the paramedics could wheel me through the back door. They pushed me into the house's back room and left me right there, since my stretcher was too awkward to steer into the dining room or living room. My family gathered around me: my brothers and sisters-in-law, Deb and Ken, my parents, Grandpa Beach, Grandma Jekabson, and, of course, Tina and Amber. They were all so happy to see me out of the hospital. Tina opened Amber's presents and mine. She'd held back many of our daughter's gifts, from the day before, so I could be there. Receiving my Christmas gifts was the most bitter part of my visit. Everyone had tried to buy me things I was interested in, like video games or clothes, but as I saw each present, I thought, *There's another thing I'll never be able to use.*

The paramedics sat outside in the ambulance for an hour and a half, and then it was time to go. That doesn't sound like long, but I was just happy to be home, to see the inside of my house. An hour and a half was more than enough. This will sound strange, but the best part of that day was the end. Not leaving the house, though I was changing enough to know that going back to the hospital was the right thing to do, but the drive itself. It was a clear day, and all the way east down Edmonton's Whitemud Freeway, I watched the sunset for the first time since the fire, through the ambulance's back window. It was the prettiest thing I'd ever seen. The colours were remarkable. Reds and oranges and yellows, all blending together. I was amazed, partly because I hadn't seen the sunset in over eight months, but also because those colours were a familiar sight. For so long, I had replayed the fire in my mind, remembering the smell of the chemical, and the smells of my hair, clothes, and flesh burning. So many times I'd thought of different things I could have done to get out of that fire faster. So many times I heard the sounds, felt my heart race, remembered the elated feeling of peace when I gave up. In all those memories, I was surrounded by intense heat penetrating deep into my body as the flames ravaged me. I saw the cause of the burns, those flames, red, yellow, and orange, swirling right in front of me. But now nature was displaying the same colours in such a beautiful way. For the entire trip back, I could see the sunset, and it put my mind in a reverie state. That sunset was one of God's creations, and it showed me that the fire didn't have to make me a victim. It showed me that with a new attitude and with the will to try, I too could transform, as the fire's colours had, into something beautiful. When I realized that, peace found me again.

Tina came to the hospital that evening, after all her guests went home. She wrote in her journal that night that I'd changed. As she walked into my room, I said, "Here comes my sunshine." I don't recall what I was thinking when I said that, but I do remember how much going home and seeing that sunset affected me. That night I reminded myself of the realizations that kept me going, and I continued to rely on those truths when I was depressed and discouraged.

The first of those truths I found in the Book of Job. Like Job, I had been blessed with all that life could offer. I'd had a great job. I made tons of money. I had a beautiful wife and a first child on the way. I had a nice house and good friends. For twenty-nine years I was blessed with good looks. And then so much of it was taken away. Like Job, I was stripped down, quite literally, since I was naked throughout my entire stay in that hospital, and afflicted with an appearance that made it difficult for my friends to look at me. I thought, *I'm being tested right now. God's allowed the devil at me.* But Job hadn't lost his faith. And neither would I.

The second realization that bolstered me was that, unlike Job, I'd been allowed to keep the most important of my blessings. Since my teens, I'd asked God for someone to love, and for enough money so I could provide for my family.

One of the first things I asked Tina, when I could finally speak, had been, "How are we doing financially?"

"We're fine," she said, and told me how much money was in our account.

"Where did all that come from?" I wondered. We'd never had that much before. It turned out to be mostly from an insurance policy I had forgotten about. God knew what would be needed and also had people generously give to us when we were in need. We even received money from someone in Japan. That took so much worry off my shoulders, to know that Tina was not in financial strife.

I had prayed for Tina's health, and for Seba, now Amber, developing in Tina's womb. I never once prayed for good looks or blond hair, or even ten fingers. I'd prayed for the things that mattered, and I now realized that God had answered those prayers.

Then I thought of my dream inside the whale's belly, and I thought back to my Bible studies with Pastor Habben, to the Book of Jonah. Even as a child, I knew this story: Jonah spends three days in the belly of a giant fish, praying. In his prayers, he says he's been to hell and back.

Jonah says: "The waters closed in over me; the deep surrounded me; weeds were wrapped around my head at the roots of the mountains." He tells God, "I went down to the land whose bars closed upon me forever; yet you brought up my life from the Pit."

I knew it was God and God alone who'd lifted me from the laundry room floor and given me the strength to try that door one more time; it was God who dragged me back from death's sweet embrace.

In Jonah's words: "As my life was ebbing away, I remembered the Lord."

• • •

They Walked Through the Valley

One warm afternoon in the summer of 2008, five years after the fire, I took Amber and Tina to a football game in Edmonton. Because it was sunny, I covered my head with a baseball cap and wore my dark sunglasses, always necessary to protect my hypersensitive eyes. I wore shorts and a tee-shirt, no longer self-conscious about the scarred, patchy skin on my arms and legs. I'd had enough of covering up and sweltering for vanity's sake. After all, there was no disguising that I was a burn survivor. I was always careful to cover my grafted skin with sunscreen, since it had no natural pigment, before I applied the moisturizer that compensated for missing oil glands.

Amber was a handful, but I loved taking her out to games and other fun activities. After buying her an Edmonton Eskimos cap and temporary tattoos, which she plastered all over her face and body, we went to get our seats.

We hadn't reached our seats before a guy stopped me to say he'd seen one of my talks. "Awesome presentation," he said. "You really change the way people think about safety. You really get through to people."

"Thanks." I shook his hand. "That's great to hear." It would never get old, hearing that my presentation had struck a chord with someone. Helping a few people think a bit differently—differently enough to avoid getting hurt like I did—let me know that my injury hadn't happened for nothing.

When we went to get hot dogs after the second quarter, another man stopped me to say the same thing. Tina was right. I was becoming famous.

We got up to leave a few minutes before the end of the game since I didn't want to get stuck in the crush with Amber, and as we made our way through the seats, I saw a guy around my age hurrying up the bleachers toward me. "Excuse me," he called out. "Are you Spencer Beach?"

That made three spottings in one outing. An all-time record.

"That's me."

"I can't believe it." The guy stared at me like a long-lost friend. I thought he might hug me. "I'm Randy," he said. "I was the paramedic that picked you up after the fire."

I grabbed Randy's outstretched hand. I couldn't believe it either! This was the face that had haunted me, the eyes that had told me just how badly I was hurt. This was the voice that talked me through the ambulance ride from the fire, keeping me conscious and talking. Randy was actually handsome; he was shorter than I was, but most people are, and fit, with a kind face. For some reason, I was surprised that he was good looking, like I used to be. I'd only remembered the pitying, frightened look in his eyes.

"I've been following your recovery through the newspaper and TV, and saw your picture," said Randy. "I read that you're a motivational speaker." I remembered that article in the *Edmonton Journal*. There'd been several stories written about me, and feature stories in the evening news, since the fire. "I couldn't believe you were alive," Randy went on. "I was so happy to read that. I never forgot you, man."

A few days after the football game, when we talked on the phone, Randy said he'd gone home that evening and told his girlfriend what happened, and then had lain awake all night, thinking about me and wondering if he could have helped me more. He'd remembered that moment after the fire, when our eyes met, as well as I had. It wasn't an experience easily forgotten. I'd been nearly naked, and I had no hair. My eyelids were already starting to contract, and my skin was charred. The unmistakable smell of burnt flesh had been almost unbearable.

In the ambulance, Randy had injected me with pain medication and kept checking my airways. Most people caught in a fire tend to breathe deeply, a panic reaction that draws fire and smoke deep into their lungs. Within minutes, the airways start to swell shut, and the victim can easily suffocate. To Randy's surprise, I continued to breathe on my own, and to speak.

He couldn't recount the ambulance ride without getting choked up. "You kept saying you didn't want your wife to see you." I'd begged him again and again to promise I would die soon.

When we arrived at the hospital, before Randy left, they put a catheter in my bladder, and my urine came out black. Whenever muscle tissue is damaged, it releases a protein called creatine kinase, and it was that protein that filtered through my kidneys into my bladder. The discolouration meant that my muscle tissue was severely, extensively damaged. Randy had never seen anything like it. He didn't think I'd make it through the night.

"Are you still a paramedic?" I asked.

"No," he said. "I'm a firefighter now."

I couldn't help but wonder if his experience with me had influenced that career change at all.

"I'm so proud of you," Randy said, before we parted.

• • •

Meeting Randy reminded me how lucky I was to have encountered all the right people when I needed help, and it also made me think about how many people the fire had affected, even beyond those closest to me. From moments after the fire, I'd had the full, unwavering attention of my parents, my wife, my brothers, and all my friends. I was all they could think about for the next year, and it was horrible. Having a child or sibling almost die, seeing him reduced to skin and bones (and not even his own skin), and then disfigured for life, scars a whole family. And of course, the person whose life was affected the most, the person who suffered the most stress and gave more of herself than she had to give, was Tina.

Four months pregnant on April 24, 2003, Tina had been shopping for our baby-to-be when she answered her cellphone to a strange woman who told her to hurry to the U of A Hospital.

"I'm with your husband," she said. "He's seriously hurt. We're waiting for an ambulance. You need to get to the hospital."

Again, Tina thought. I'd been hurt on the job, again. More frustrated than frightened, Tina headed for the University of Alberta Hospital. She got there before me and was standing at the nurses' window, trying to get more information and filling out paperwork to get me admitted, when she heard someone say, "The 90 percent burn is here."

That's when she started to panic. She could only stand and watch as my stretcher flew by. The body on that stretcher was shrouded by a sheet, except for one arm. My arm.

Tina grabbed her cellphone to call Craig's wife, Sandra, who was not only her sister-in-law but also a close friend. Tina knew she could count on Sandra to round up the rest of the family. But when Sandra answered, Tina found herself crying too hard to speak. "Spencer's hurt," she managed to say.

Sandra was on her way home from work, standing in the grocery store. She asked what happened.

"Spencer ..." Tina couldn't get the words out. The nurse by her side took Tina's phone and explained the situation to Sandra. Sandra immediately contacted Craig and then Reagan. Since my parents didn't answer their phone, she picked up Craig and they drove to my parents' house.

"Spencer's been hurt," Sandra told my mother. "We're on our way to the hospital."

Before they left, my mother called Pastor Habben, who was in the middle of supper with his wife and three young daughters.

"Spencer's done it again," my mother said.

"What happened, Andrea?"

"He was in a fire. An explosion."

Back at the hospital, a nurse led Tina to a private room, where she waited alone for an hour. She contacted her parents and Marc. A few of my friends from work, who'd already heard what happened, arrived at the ER. A small crowd gathered.

They didn't know yet exactly how dire things were, but as my mother says, you know it's bad when you get to the hospital and find two doctors, two nurses, and the chaplain waiting for you.

When Pastor Habben arrived, he comforted my loved ones as best he could. "I don't understand the mind of God," he said, "but I do know that God is with us and will not abandon us. Let's remember Psalm 23. 'The Lord is my shepherd,' he prayed. 'Even though I walk through the valley of the shadow of death, I will fear no evil; you are with me; your rod and your staff, they comfort me.'"

• • •

While my family prayed and waited, Dr. Prichard gave me the choice to fight or to die. He'd been called down from the burn unit to Emergency because he was the doctor on call. The doctor working that night thought my injury was too large, and that I should receive compassionate care. That I should be allowed to die. Most hospitals in North America, and in the world, would have made that decision with no hesitation, but I had landed in one of the best burn units in the country, led by one of the best doctors.

To this day, Dr. Prichard is the best doctor I've ever met. He has the nicest bedside manner, and he is extremely wise. He's genuinely caring, because he knows what his patients will go through; he understands the pain and the difficulties. His demeanour is laid back and quiet; you can tell he reflects on everything he hears and observes. His only flaw is that he cheers for the wrong football team—the Saskatchewan Roughriders. Before one of my hand surgeries, when I was on the mend, I wrote the Edmonton Eskimos "EE" logo right where Dr. P. was going to operate.

When Dr. Prichard gave me the option to live or die, he did it knowing the best thing for me might be death. He's told me he pondered whether he should even give me the choice for treatment. I would present one of the most challenging cases the unit had ever faced, plus they'd just had a burn patient die, so morale was low. Some of the nurses and therapists believed I would suffer too much, that they, personally, would not want to live with burns as severe as mine, and wouldn't want to face the treatment. But I had good social support and I had patches of uninjured skin. I was young and, strange as it sounds, I was in great health. And Tina was pregnant. That was the clincher.

Normally, Tina would have had to decide whether I should receive treatment or compassionate care, but I was still lucid enough to make the decision myself. I'm grateful that it was my own decision, and it will always be on my shoulders, not hers. I wouldn't have wanted her to live with the doubt that would inevitably follow whichever decision she made. When I chose to fight, Dr. Prichard knew my chances of survival were small, and he was concerned that the stress could cause Tina to miscarry or suffer other complications. He warned her that if I did survive, my quality of life would be greatly diminished. According to his experience, I would likely never work again, would lose my friends and family, and would spend my sad, short life restricted to a lonely house with climate control.

But I didn't hesitate. I wanted to get better, and Dr. P. was ready to do his best. He had the nurses from the burn unit come down. He had to get enough people on board to try to help me, and they had to start immediately.

• • •

At the accident scene, a small crowd was still gathered. When the ambulance pulled away, we'd left a group of shocked neighbours and tradespeople, a fire truck, and a police car. The firefighters discovered there was nothing they could do. The blaze, a typical flash fire, hadn't lasted much longer than the time it took to incinerate my life as I knew it. When Vail and his brother arrived, along with Jack's wife, who was on her way to check on me when the explosion happened, they saw the basement windows blown out where the furnace had exploded, and a charred mess inside the garage. They had no way of knowing just how badly I was hurt.

Shortly after that, Casey Leahey and Robyn Wagenseil arrived from Occupational Health and Safety to investigate the scene. They were always alerted when the police or fire department was called to a work-related accident site. Casey, whom I was destined to meet many times, was a big man who emanated caring and competence with his deep voice and strong personality.

Casey and Robyn took photographs throughout the house. They photographed the scorched floor, the many empty 901 containers I'd set aside, the now blackened walls, my tool boxes, my glasses lying on the floor, and my knee pads and shoes, which saved some of my skin from burning. The paramedics had left those in the garage. Down in the basement, Casey and Robyn photographed the bent, distorted furnace and ducts. The investigation revealed that the fire had started when the temperature inside the house fell below that indicated on the thermostat. The furnace had switched on, sucking air and 901 fumes into its belly. In a second, the fireball reached the ground floor, which was full of the fumes from my day's work. And I was standing right in the middle of them, with 901 splattered on my skin. Those fumes were even in my lungs.

Richard, the trades guy who left the house before the fire, had already spoken with the constables.

"What did you see?" Casey asked Richard.

"I'd just walked to the curb," said Richard. "I heard a muffled explosion. Low and vibrating, and the whole ground shook. I turned around, and it was the most intense flames I'd ever seen. The front door had a little side panel in it, and all I could see was this immense flame going from floor to ceiling." He struggled for words to describe it. "You know the way the flame on a gas barbeque is? It was like that. Forced up." Richard's first instinct had been to phone 911, which he did, immediately.

I couldn't understand for the longest time why Richard hadn't turned back to help me. I pictured him standing outside the house, just watching it burn, knowing I was trapped inside and letting me stay there. Now I know he could feel the fire's heat from the sidewalk, and there was no way he could have approached the house without imperiling his life. Also, it just happened so fast. He stared into the garage, phone in hand, in shock, and almost immediately he noticed the flames moving. He looked closer, and realized he was seeing limbs. He was seeing me.

"All of a sudden, he just jumped out," said Richard. He described how I rolled in the dirt to put out the flames, and how the neighbour sprayed me down. "All that was left on him was his underwear and socks." I was actually wearing my work belt and boots. No surprise that Richard's memory of the incident was a little blurred.

"Are you going to be okay?" Casey asked.

"Yeah," said Richard. "I've got another job to do."

Richard headed to a house in another new development, and when he arrived, he sat down on the front porch. He sat there for the next four hours. The sound of the explosion echoed in his ears. The sensation of the sidewalk shaking under his feet. Again and again, he saw my body falling, in flames, from the inside garage door. He saw the shreds of fabric, which had once been my clothes, smoking, flames still playing over them as I lay in the dirt screaming. He'd been seconds from suffering the same fate.

Richard never did go inside and do his work that day, and for years, he wouldn't get through a day without thinking about the fire. He wouldn't get through a night without confronting it in his dreams. Like Randy, Richard assumed I would die, and when he read about me in the newspaper a year and a half later, he was ecstatic. Sitting on that porch after the fire, he was sure he'd witnessed the last moments of my life.

• • •

Back at the hospital, my family was beginning to realize they were probably about to lose me.

"Spencer's injury is severe," Dr. Prichard told my wife, parents, and brothers. "He's chosen treatment, but his chances are not good."

A police officer came in to explain what had happened, and he handed Tina my wedding ring.

Dr. P. would tell me, eventually, how painful it had been for him, telling Tina I might die while she was pregnant; since she always believed I'd pull through, it may have been a worse moment for him than it was for her. He gave my family the same devastating news he'd just given me. "Spencer has a 5 percent chance to live." Then he asked what they wanted him to do.

"What does Spencer want?" my mother asked.

"He wants us to fight for his life."

Neither my parents nor Tina ever questioned my decision. My mother remembers saying in her head, *You know what, God? It's all yours. You have to carry this, because it's too heavy for me.*

Dr. P. urged my wife and parents to see me, but only Tina and my mother went with him to my room. My father's own mother, sick with hepatitis, had fallen into a coma when he was twenty. He saw her in the hospital before she died, and had always regretted it. That diminished version of his mother, on her deathbed, had overwhelmed his memories of who she really was, and he didn't want the same thing to happen with me. That's why he stayed away from the hospital until I was conscious. I had the same worries, and had begged Dr. P. not to let Tina and my parents see me. Fortunately, he didn't listen to me. After all, he knew this might be the last chance we had to say our goodbyes.

After Dr. Prichard's prognosis, Tina and my mother expected me to look like the living dead, and I actually looked better than they anticipated. Third and fourth degree burns don't look red and sore like a surface burn; the skin looks white or blackish, and the proteins in the skin coagulate, giving it a leathery appearance and texture. Tina stepped through the doorway and stopped. Most of my body was covered with a sheet, but she could see that my face was puffy, and I had no hair. I saw her standing in the doorway, her face serious, fighting the emotion. She was absorbing the impact of what met her eyes, and holding back her tears.

"Cancel the RRSPs," I told her.

She nodded.

I explained how she could get my next paycheque and cash it, and how to access our investments. I was in such a panic about the money and the details, because I wanted to make sure she could take care of herself, that I forgot to tell her I loved her.

"Can I touch him?" Tina asked.

Two nurses helped her into the room, and I cringed. I didn't want anyone touching me. I was sure my skin would slough off like the charred coating of a roasted marshmallow.

Tina stood close, her blonde hair falling over her shoulders. I could see the slight bulge of her pregnant belly.

"He's not burned here," said Dr. Prichard.

Although I remember her touching my forehead, Tina has always insisted it was the back of my neck. As a man, I am sure I am wrong! Either way, she touched me to let me know that she wasn't going anywhere. That everything would be all right.

My mother remembers watching this scene and thinking I didn't seem so badly hurt after all. My face looked fine, except for the black specks stuck all over it. She'd seen burn survivors before, and was relieved to see my face wouldn't be disfigured. Weeks later, when the doctors removed my bandages, she would be shocked.

• • •

Tina and my mother returned to the family and to the gathering crowd of friends, and Dr. Prichard offered my brothers a chance to see me. Reagan hadn't been too concerned when my mother phoned him, crying, saying I'd been hurt. I'd already come through so many injuries and accidents, he thought I was like Bruce Willis's character, who walks away from train wrecks and car crashes unscathed, in the movie *Unbreakable*. "I figured next you'd probably be electrocuted," he told me, once we were able to joke again.

But when he saw how stricken Tina and my mother looked, he knew this fire had been no ordinary mishap.

Reagan steeled himself, but Craig didn't want to see me so badly hurt. Sandra told him, "You might never see your brother again. You'd regret it for the rest of your life." Craig was afraid my father was right, that he'd pointlessly tarnish his memories of me. But he was more afraid that Sandra was right, and that he'd miss his last chance to see me alive.

Dr. Prichard led my brothers to my room.

Despite Tina and my mother's impressions of my appearance, Reagan and Craig were both so horrified, they suffered from nightmares in the nights that followed, and still sometimes do. I have no memory of their presence. By then I was wrapped head to foot in bandages, was losing consciousness, and my face and body had swollen enormously. When I'd made the choice to fight, the burn team started fighting for me immediately. They inserted a feeding tube and a ventilator and started filling my veins with fluid, so much so that within twenty hours I swelled from my usual 170 pounds to 240 pounds. That was the only way to counter the dehydration that would have otherwise killed me, if infection didn't get to me first.

Reagan eventually told me, "You're lucky you didn't have to see yourself that day. You don't know how lucky you are. It was the worst thing I ever saw.

And I'll never get the smell out of my head."

In his memory, the body lying there looked like a charcoal-briquetted corpse. It had no eyelids (actually, my eyelids had contracted, not burned off) so its eyes jutted out like golf balls. Its lips were pulled back, teeth bared. The body looked like something that had been dead for years—only it was struggling to breathe, drawing in air in shallow, shuddering gasps. Reagan and Craig tried to say a prayer, but they couldn't. After a few seconds, Craig turned and left. Reagan lasted another minute.

After that, Reagan spent two days on his garage floor with a pack of smokes and a bottle of whisky. He sobbed and howled and sat in stunned silence. He couldn't get the image of that breathing corpse out of his head. He just couldn't believe that thing was human, let alone that it was his little brother. After those two days, he took his smokes and booze inside, and moved to the basement couch, where he remained for another ten days.

"One day there was a knock on my door," he told me, "and when I opened it, the whole neighbourhood was there." Reagan remembers standing there in his bathrobe, probably stinking, as an endless line of neighbours flooded past him into his home, each bearing a dish of home-cooked food.

Craig reacted more quietly, also turning to alcohol. He couldn't bring himself to return to the hospital, and was tormented by nightmares every time he slept. Both Kelly and Sandra struggled to support their husbands through their grief and horror. They both did their best, but they knew they couldn't erase what my brothers had seen. A month or two passed before Reagan and Craig visited me again, and now, instead of a blackened corpse, they found a slightly more palatable horror-movie archetype: a mummy. A mummy hooked up by tubes to a multitude of machines.

Reagan's depression lasted a year and a half. Again and again, he retreated to the garage and sat there for hours, crying. He wouldn't talk to anyone during those dark times, and Kelly didn't know what to do to help him. My nephews took it hard, too, especially Tyler, who was twelve. He visited me a couple of times, even though Reagan and Kelly warned him about my state and appearance. It really bothered him that this had happened to his favourite uncle, and he became depressed and defiant. My accident happened during a vulnerable time in his life, and he had a tough few years.

When I speak with trades crews now, I emphasize how, by hurting myself, I hurt everyone I loved. Irresponsible and reckless practices are not only dangerous, but selfish. Six years later, I've found my way through my own pain. I am very proud of who I am and what I have accomplished, but to forgive myself for the pain I put my loved ones through—I still haven't found a way to do that. I can never take back the horrific hours my family spent in that hospital, I can never erase the nightmare images from my brothers' minds, and I can never compensate Tina for what she went through. And it was about to get a lot worse before it got better.

• • •

Stripped Down

For the first few days, while surgeons cut away all my destroyed tissue, my family waited. My mother spent the day after the accident answering phone call after phone call. Then she was at the hospital every day, unless she caught a cold, since any virus could have killed me. Sandra took the week off work and spent all her time at the hospital with Tina.

She didn't have to explain to her boss what had happened; she just phoned and said, "You know that man on the news, who was in the explosion? That was my brother-in-law."

Reagan's employer had recognized my name in the newscast and didn't expect to see my brother for some time. Craig was the only one who went to work the day after the accident.

Our friends and family rallied around Tina. From the night of the accident, Tina was never alone. Her parents, sisters, and friends made up a schedule so there was always someone in the house with her at night. Marc cut grass that summer and shovelled snow when the time came, and he and his girlfriend, Janice, who was soon his fiancée and then his wife, even took care of Amber after she was born.

• • •

Once I had donor and artificial skin in place, my chances were much better, but to anyone except a doctor, I looked worse. A lot worse. As some of my eloquent loved ones tell me, I looked like a monster, even with most of my body wrapped in bandages. The first time my sister-in-law Kelly came to see me, she looked through the window into my room and froze, afraid of what she saw. She admits she refused to enter the room. She just couldn't do it. Throughout the months that followed, friends came and looked through the window. Some, like Jay, sat with me for a few minutes, but others left, unable to face me. Unable to process that what they saw *was* me. I can hardly blame them. I didn't know what I looked like in those days, but now that I've seen the photographs, I can imagine wanting to run away myself.

Skin normally has three layers, and while I waited for my skin grafts, I only had the bottom layer. As Dr. P. explained it, I had the rafters but no shingles. My skin was red and transparent. According to Marc, I looked like a Body Works exhibit, as though someone had peeled off all my skin and put plastic wrap in its place. The first time Tina saw me without bandages, no one warned her. She just walked into the room, saw me, and forced herself not to turn back.

She willed herself to stay in that room because she didn't want to let me down. Although I was still sedated, she believed I could sense her presence, and that I'd know, on some level, if she recoiled from me in horror. Needless to say, Tina was traumatized that day, though she didn't realize how much in the moment, and wouldn't until years later. She was running on adrenalin, with no time or energy to contemplate the extremity of her situation or even to feel sorry for herself.

If the picture isn't frightening enough already, I was covered in splints and other apparatuses that kept my body in "anti-deformity position." With any healing skin, the scar tissue contracts. Even with a small cut, you can see the skin around the edges tightening. Now imagine the effect of that tightening on 90 percent of a body. The tendency after a big burn is to curl into the fetal position, and, without intervention, a patient stays in that position forever, unable to move. Splints kept me spread-eagle with all my joints straight and my feet pointing up, so I'd eventually be able to stand again. I couldn't have a pillow because the skin on my neck would contract, pulling my chin down toward my collarbone.

Although I felt completely defeated for months, convinced I wasn't getting better, I realize now how incredibly lucky I was. If I'd been burnt in a country without Canada's resources, and somehow survived, I would have been spared the long, painful, grotesque-looking, and seemingly futile therapy. And I would have spent the rest of my miserable life curled into a ball, unable to move. There's a reason some of my caregivers and friends have dubbed me the Million Dollar Man. Sharon has described to me burn units in less developed countries, without workers' compensation, public health care, and cutting edge medical training and resources, and I can only pray for those burn survivors whose lives will never resume like mine has.

I arrived at the hospital, and within twenty-four hours, Sharon began physical therapy by assessing all my joints. From then on, she assessed every joint in my body every day, five days a week. Then she did my stretches. It took one or two hours each time. Physical therapists, like Sharon, do stretches and range-of-motion work, while occupational therapists, like Diana, work on feeding, grabbing things, putting on clothes, and otherwise regaining independent function. For a patient like me, in the beginning, Diana's work overlaps Sharon's. Diana worked on positioning my hands and arms with splints so I'd eventually be able to use them again.

I have to mention here that burn doctors, nurses, and therapists are a special breed. Most medical professionals beg to leave the unit within months, or even after a few shifts, and many have reported gaining weight and sleeping better after transferring to a less stressful part of the hospital. That goes for surgeons as well. The vast majority of plastic surgeons use their skills for cosmetic procedures. It's a lot easier to make breasts bigger and noses straighter than to replace a patient's skin.

And I definitely would not have regained my life the way I have without a man called Dr. Steven Boyce of the Cincinnati Children's Hospital, who dedicated his life's work and research to helping people with massive burns like mine. Burn patients like me used to die, almost inevitably, of infection. When antibiotics made survival possible at all, massive burn patients had all their burnt skin replaced with "autografts." The surgeons shaved a layer of skin from an unburned area of the patient's own body and transplanted it to the wound site. Each site then had only one layer of skin and both had to heal, the donor site—the place where the unburned skin was harvested—often even more slowly and painfully than the graft. My feet and groin only had so much skin to give and would have had to heal before they could be harvested again—and again and again.

But Dr. Boyce's process requires harvesting only a business-card-sized skin sample. He puts the cells in a special solution and grows 100 three-by-three-inch sheets of full-thickness skin with the patient's own genetic makeup, so the body doesn't reject it like cadaver skin or artificial skin. With 1 percent of a patient's skin, Dr. Boyce can grow enough "cultured skin substitute" to cover the whole body. Luckily for me, just as I was burned, Dr. Boyce was conducting clinical trials outside Cincinnati to show he could export the technology. I became his guinea pig. Forty-five percent of my body was grafted with cultured skin substitute, grown in Cincinnati and shipped back to Edmonton. Dr. P. and his team sent skin cells from my feet and groin in early May, and in early June, Dr. Boyce started sending back patches for grafting. When Dr. P. harvested skin on my left foot for Dr. Boyce, it left a divot that's still there to this day. I have named that divot "Linda" after my physical therapist in the Glenrose Hospital.

To this day, the majority of my abdomen and chest and three-quarters of my right arm and my legs show the distinctive whiteness of Dr. Boyce's cultured skin. I received autografts on almost half my body. The first surgery I endured was on my back. The surgeons stretched the viable skin by punching it full of tiny holes and pulling it like mesh to three times its original size. They knew I would be on my back for a long time so covering this area with skin was of utmost importance. My back is now covered in hundreds of tiny, evenly spaced, diamond-shaped scars. I call my back my "Christmas ham," as it resembles the outer layer of a packaged ham at the grocery store.

"There'll be a fair amount of scarring, and it won't look normal," Dr. P. told my family of the cultured skin substitute. "The new skin won't have pigment, hair, or sweat glands. But it's durable and it's lasting, and if all goes well, he'll be alive."

The time it took to get me covered was about two-thirds less than it would have been without Dr. Boyce's method, if they'd managed to keep me alive at all. I would have spent two years at the U of A Hospital, rather than nine months. So from a psychiatric point of view, the impact of being sick for a long time was much less. I did even better than Dr. P. expected, and healed faster.

My treatment with CSS was a clinical trial. There is now a patent on the culturing process, and no one else will receive it in Canada until the FDA approves it. I was incredibly lucky that my accident happened where and when it did, and the U of A burn unit was lucky, too, that they got to use Dr. Boyce's method during that small window when circumstances allowed it.

• • •

My mother, and especially Tina, spent as much time with me as they could. My dad spent two days just praying. He didn't doubt that God had let this happen to me; everything that happens to a Christian happens for a reason. He tried to get his head around it—he had to accept that the matter was in God's hands.

After those two days, my father had to get back to work, running the farmers' market business so my mother could be with me. Despite the strain on their own well-being, my loved ones just did what they had to do. Every day for the first weeks, the nurses reminded Tina and my mother I might not survive. Every day, as fingertips, whole fingers, parts of my nose, and my ears proved unviable, the surgeons cut them away in order to save my life.

"The parts of the body that stick out always get the worst of it in a fire," Rudi explained.

As more and more of my extremities were cut away, and it became less and less clear whether I'd ever wake up, and whether I'd be brain damaged if I did, the nurses predicted that Tina's constant presence would wane. They warned my mother that one day soon there'd be a wedding ring and maybe a note on my pillow, and Tina would be gone. But that day never came. All through her pregnancy, and then with a newborn to care for, she was at my side. When other family members and friends visited me, they invariably found Tina either in my room with me, or just down the hall at the nurses' station. She ate her meals in the hospital cafeteria.

My mother was amazed by how strong Tina was, and how attentive to me. You can only talk to someone in a coma for so long before you run out of things to say, so Tina made notes during all her phone conversations. She passed a little notebook around the waiting room so all the people who weren't allowed in my room could give me messages, and then she read them all to me. She always told me who'd come to visit, and when.

One night, the burn unit phoned Tina and told her to come in. "Spencer's blood work is really bad," Rudi explained. "High CO_2 levels. Sky high." In fact, Rudi had never seen a live person with such bad arterial blood gases. They had to phone Dr. P., who gave me muscle relaxants to completely paralyze my body. Through the ventilator, they gave me as much oxygen as they could. "If he survives, he could have brain damage," Rudi had to tell Tina. "And I'm sorry, but he might not make it through the night."

Tina has told me she put on a brave face before entering my room. Then she stood by my bed and gave me hell. "You can't die," she told me. "You have too much to live for. You need to come home. You need to live so you can be a father to our child."

I believe it was that night I dreamed I was dying. I only remember one dream like that, where I was at the end of my life. I'd been part of a massive intergalactic battle, but that was over, and I was alone on a big asteroid. I was the only person left, forgotten in a cave inside a crater on a rock floating out in space, billions of light years from any source of light, let alone life. All I could see were grey and black shapes. I huddled there, cold and hungry and unable to do anything for myself, and I knew there was no way out. I was going to die, and I was terrified. I felt myself getting colder and colder, and weaker and weaker.

Then, out of nowhere, a huge spaceship appeared. They beamed me up on board and took me out of that place. The people on that ship saved my life.

When I learned that Tina had come into my room and told me firmly all the reasons I had to live, I remembered my dream. I believe the spaceship swooped into my dream when I heard Tina's voice, bringing hope when I'd already given up, lifting me out of the cave, out of the crater, and telling me I was not alone in the universe.

Tina told me everything I had to live for, and she ended her rant in tears. She knew I might not have the strength to continue. "If you have to go," she told me, "I'll understand."

I was already on my way back.

• • •

Tina and my mother spent long, frustrating hours trying to communicate with me with the communication board, and then my ventilator came out, but I could hardly be bothered to speak. Though some of my therapists and nurses commented on my politeness considering the circumstances, I know I was a real bastard to those around me. I sent visitors away, telling them I didn't want to see them. Kelly gathered her courage to visit me eight months after the fire, and I asked her to leave because I didn't want her to see me eating without bending my elbows, with the two-foot-long forks my nurse attached to cuffs around my hands. Marc remembers driving to see me, many times, only to meet with a look that said, *Get out of here; I don't want to talk to you.*

When I speak about self-pity, depression, and anger, I ask my audiences if they've ever walked past a yard that was weedy, with uncut grass, overflowing garbage cans, and a fence with rotten, peeling boards.

"Did you bother to stop and look for something nice?" I ask. "Or did you keep going, maybe saying something insulting about the yard and its keeper? No one will stop if they see nothing beautiful to stop for. They'll brush you off and move on to more pleasant things."

But of course, my case back in the hospital was slightly different, because no matter how nasty I was, the nurses and doctors kept coming back. Some of my friends and relatives came less and less often, but Tina kept coming every day, no matter how I treated her. And I've come to realize my behaviour was even worse than my memory tells me. Tina kept three journals during my recovery. Every day, she documented her observations, any progress I'd made, and my behaviour. Five years after the fire, she gave me the last of those journals, the one she wrote while I was at the end of my stay at the U of A Hospital. I was surprised and dismayed by some of what I read.

I remembered that when people came to see me, I often pretended to be asleep so I wouldn't have to speak with them; my mother used to read to me anyway, because she knew I was faking. What I don't remember is doing this to Tina. I recall falling asleep in earnest when Tina was reading to me or speaking to me because I was too exhausted to engage with her; but according to her journal, she often left the room when I fell asleep, only to look back through the window and realize I was awake after all.

When she let me read her journal, it was too late to tell her how her visits, and my mother's, were the only things that made me happy back then. I realized from reading Tina's account that I never showed any appreciation for her presence at all. That's appalling considering Tina spent so much time in that hospital that the nurses threw a baby shower for her. I remember the event well: I was wheeled into the room, on my bed, but I knew I shouldn't be there. I couldn't move, I was uncomfortable, and I was grumpy. The last place I wanted to be was in a room full of joyful, cheerful nurses. They invited me to cheer me up, but I was bored, and I wanted to get back to my room, to be bored there instead.

"Rudi," I whispered, getting the attention of the only other man in the room. "Get me out of here!"

"What's the matter?" Rudi asked, as he pushed me from the room.

"Baby showers are for girls," I said.

"Oh, Spencer," Rudi laughed. I guess he didn't mind witnessing that scene.

"It's just chatter," I said. "Girls like to sit around and chatter. I'm a *guy*. Guys get out and do things."

It would be a long time before this guy got out to do anything.

After Amber was born, Tina often left her with a babysitter, or with the nurses. I wondered and asked where my daughter was, but according to Tina's journal, I showed little interest. "He never asks to see her," she wrote. I couldn't believe it when I read that, because all I remembered was the excitement I felt about being a father, and the amazement that filled me when I saw my daughter for the first time. I did want to see her, but I didn't ask the right questions.

According to Tina's journal, she brought Amber into the room one day, and couldn't stop her crying. "Spencer talked to her, and settled her down." Tina wrote about how emotional that was for her. "That's the first time he really spoke to her."

It filled me with shame to read, in my wife's words, how I wished her goodnight each evening before she went home, only to insist, a couple of hours later, that the nurses ask her to come back. Just as Tina was finishing her dinner, or taking a few well-deserved moments on her own comfortable sofa in the company of her parents, the phone would ring.

"Spencer wants to see you," the voice on the other end would say apologetically. "He says he needs to speak with you."

Only once, Tina agreed to come back, on the condition that I stay awake until she got there. When she arrived, I was fast asleep.

• • •

One day as my mother watched me lying sedated and drugged, tubes in my mouth, nose, veins, and chest, unrecognizable as her son, she thought to herself, for a fleeting moment, *Why are we keeping him alive*? As far as she could see, I was unaware at best and suffering at worst. I was so far down, she couldn't picture me up and walking and talking as the doctors said I would. And if I did recover, the doctors had warned her, I would never be the way I had been. I would probably never work; never contribute anything to the world. Even worse, I would never be happy.

But my mother remembered her faith, and found it in herself to believe I was still there. She was afraid she wouldn't be able to handle losing her good-looking son and having a child disfigured with burn scars, but now she says she saw me improve so much that I don't look so disfigured to her. She just sees that I'm living my life, that I'm still lovable and fun. She says she understands why God let this happen, and kept me alive. I did recover, and she has her son back. A different son, whom she would never have had otherwise. And I have something to offer the world. My mother always said that God works things out for those who love Him. And the things I've done with my life, she says, have brought blessings to many people.

I was blessed that my loved ones never gave up on me and kept fighting on my behalf, because as I came out of my coma and slowly realized what had happened to me, I began, slowly but surely, to give up on myself.

• • •

Facing Up

After Amber was born, I decided to tell someone about the accident. I still hadn't revealed to anyone that I remembered it. Maybe it was because Reagan had also inherited our mother's near-photographic memory that I decided to tell him my worst memory before I told anyone else. Maybe it was just because he often came to the hospital on his lunch break and sat by my bedside.

Reagan and I had always been similar, though he was smarter than I was—I'm sure he'd score higher on an IQ test—and less rambunctious. I thought of my brother when I learned about van Gogh, the painter whose genius drove him to cut off his own ear. Some people are so smart, they drive themselves crazy; they think and they analyze, and they can't stop. That tormenting intelligence, along with the family responsibilities he'd taken on so early in life, contributed to Reagan's serious demeanour. He was taking my accident hard. I wouldn't know until later just how much it affected him.

The day I chose to tell Reagan about the fire, I lay silently throughout his visit, waiting for the right moment, until he took out a cigarette and his lighter and placed them neatly on the table between us. That meant he was about to leave.

"Reagan," I said.

"Yeah, Spence?"

"I remember the fire."

My brother looked at me with his steady, bright blue gaze, his elbows resting on his thighs.

"I remember every detail," I said. "Do you want to know?"

Reagan looked away. He shook his head.

"Yes," he said. "But not right now. I have to go back to work. I'll come back after five, and you can tell me then."

I spent the afternoon rehearsing in my head what I'd tell my brother, from the other tradesman stepping over me on his way out the door to the paramedic leaning over me, telling me without speaking that life, at least as I knew it, was over for me. I remembered the moments when I lay hunched on the floor, waiting for death. When I was little, I used to stop sometimes, walking home from school in the spring, to lie on the warm grass and watch the sky. Sometimes an hour would pass, and I wouldn't even notice it. That feeling was the closest I could come to describing the reverie I experienced in that burning house, when I gave up. The calm I could have entered for eternity, instead of facing these plodding months of suffering. I didn't know yet why it wasn't time for me to go, but I was doing my best to trust that God had His reasons.

When Reagan came back that evening, I told him everything. It was the first of thousands of times I'd tell that story; I'd go on to tell it in front of hundreds and thousands of people, several times a week. But telling Reagan that first time was one of the hardest things I'd ever done. I knew I was hurting him with my words, forcing him to see the same images that tormented me day after day. But I needed to tell him, and he needed to hear it.

After I told Reagan, I told Tina. Like my brother, she didn't want to know, but at the same time, she did. Neither of them wanted to face the ordeal of hearing it, but they braced themselves, for my sake. It was a week later that Tina said two Occupational Health and Safety officers wanted to interview me. She told me how those officers had investigated the scene right after the fire, and had interviewed all the witnesses. If I could describe the fire, it would help them immensely with their case. I agreed, and a few days later, a man named Casey and a woman named Robyn came to see me.

"Nothing you say will be used against you," Casey assured me, before they began their questions. "You didn't do anything wrong."

They asked me to describe my responsibilities as a service guy, and to explain why I was sent to Robertson Close the day of the fire. Then they asked me to describe the day in as much detail as I could, like I'd done for Reagan and Tina.

"Okay," said Casey, when I finished. "I'm going to ask you some questions about safety training. Have you ever heard the term WHMIS?"

"Yes."

"Do you know what that stands for?"

"No."

He went on to ask about Roberts 1901, and how we used it to remove linoleum. Before they left, they told me again that I hadn't done anything wrong.

When Casey and Robyn assured me that I was blameless in the accident, they were trying to support me. Unfortunately, their well-meant words fed the parasites of self-pity and anger that had lodged in my mind. When I replayed the interview in my head, it was obvious what those OH&S investigators thought. Casey had dwelled a bit on the fact that I hadn't been trained in WHMIS, which turned out to stand for Workplace Hazardous Materials Information System, and was compulsory training for workers dealing with dangerous chemicals. I had been hurt because no one had bothered to train me. Even my father had never trained me at Beach Brothers because he and his own father hadn't known about safety protocols. Jack, also, had neglected his moral and legal duty to prepare me. *I was a victim.*

I eventually read Casey's report for OH&S, and it was strange to see all the details, recorded so bluntly. The deciding moments of my life were summed up in one sentence: "The ensuing flames engulfed the Top Floor worker, who was able to make his way into the garage via the inside door leading into the garage."

Since Amber's birth, my anger had dissipated a lot. I'd moved toward forgiving all the people who'd contributed to my injury, and I had regained my trust in God. But now all the anger came back. I was the one lying flat on my back as every single person who'd ignored their responsibilities went about their lives, probably thinking of me rarely, if ever. My days stretched out again into torturous movies inside my head, of how I could have been saved from the fire if only this person or that person had made a better decision.

But then, slowly, it began to dawn on me: there was someone I was forgetting to blame. Myself. I could have made different decisions, too. I could have changed my own fate, just by doing a few things differently. I'd replayed the day of the fire thousands of times in my mind, and now I replayed it as it should have happened. I should have turned off the furnace completely, not just turned it down. Sure, I was only doing what Jack said, but I'd known most furnaces have a simple on-off switch beside them. I'd been too lazy to walk down the stairs and take that extra precaution. One little switch, and there would have been no fire. I could have read the Material Safety Data Sheet for Roberts 1901, or even the fine print on the container. I had worked with that chemical so many times and had never bothered to read the label. I'd chosen not to jam the house's doors open just so I could avoid cleaning a twenty-dollar hammer.

And my gloves! The thought of those leather gloves out in the truck may be what tortured me most. Rudi gave me a new way of looking at my disfigured fingers when he told me that some fire survivors don't have burns on their hands. "Those are the people that don't fight," he said. "People that are suicidal. People who fight always have bad hand burns."

Because of my overwhelming desire to live, I'd gripped a white-hot door handle; I'd sacrificed my fingers for my life. But that didn't change the fact that my gloves would almost certainly have saved my hands, the same way my boots saved my feet and my belt saved my groin. People look at me and see my disfigured face, but if I could have one thing back, it would be my fingers. The deformities feel normal to me after what I've been through, and although some people can't handle my appearance or accept my scars, most people get over the burns quickly once they realize a real person, full of life, is inside. The loss of my fingers is what truly affects my life. Some of the simplest tasks have become great challenges. Although I have found ways to overcome and adapt to my hands as they are now, I miss being able to snap my fingers, grip a glass or container, or button up my pants fast. Little losses I couldn't have imagined until they happened to me.

During my medically induced coma, I'd dreamed of a contraption that fired shotguns. My friends and I were having a blast, firing shots into the air, until one guy was accidentally shot. I remembered the dismay that settled over me in that dream after the laughter stopped. I had been laughing along with everyone else. I knew what that dream meant: I'd been reckless. I hadn't taken my own safety seriously. And it went beyond that. By not bothering to ensure my safety, I hadn't taken my life seriously, and I had played carelessly with the well-being of everyone I cared about.

Jack had been my mentor, and he'd taught me a lot. The most important lesson I'd learned from him was to admit when I was wrong. Now I realized I'd learned something else from Jack: how stupid it was to follow orders blindly. Finally, I told myself, *I did some things that day that weren't so smart. It was me who failed to turn off the furnace. It was me who agreed to use that chemical that way, and it was me who failed to get my gloves. It was me who failed to jam open the door. It was me who followed orders blindly. It was me who put Jack's work ahead of my family's interests. Let's face it. I could have said no to Jack. If I'd refused to do the job in that way, the fire would never have happened.*

I thought about the other people I'd blamed. The homebuilder had allowed this process to happen, knowing full well how we removed linoleum. And all of the homebuilders we worked for did the same. I also was extremely angry with Richard for a long time. I couldn't understand, when I played the fire over and over again in my head, lying in my uncomfortable hospital bed, immobile and in great pain, why he never came to my rescue. Why he never opened that front door for me! Richard was the last person I managed to forgive and the one who deserved it the most. I now realize that if Richard had tried to help me, two families would have been hurt that day, not just one. In fact, if I saw him today, I would shake his hand and thank him for preserving his family from the pain mine has faced.

Amazingly enough, taking responsibility for what happened filled me with optimism and new strength. Releasing myself from blaming others was the first step I needed to take on the mental journey to rebuilding a fragmented life. My life. As Pastor Habben often reminded me, God doesn't want bad things for us. The Book of Genesis tells us we must suffer throughout our lives, but God also said: "I won't give you more than you can bear." My parents always taught me that God makes all things work out for the good; otherwise He wouldn't be God. To free myself from anger, and to embrace God's love and promises, it was time to put my faith in Him wholeheartedly. It was time to let Him show me how this wasn't more than I could handle. How He could make it work out for the best. I challenged God. I said: *You allowed this to happen. You said you wouldn't give me more than I could bear. How are you going to turn this around for the good? My future is in your hands,* I told him. *You make this better, because I don't have the strength to do it alone.* And I knew He would. What happened from then on, how my life grew and continues to grow, has made me realize the awesome power of God and how His blessings far outweigh my faith.

I remembered again what Jack had taught me about mistakes, and the next thing I told myself was, *I forgive you, Spence*. And I meant it.

As soon as I did that, the rest of my anger disappeared, and so did my psychic pain. In its place was only desire. Desire to get better.

• • •

Back to the Glenrose

Throughout four months of lying on my back, moving toward forgiveness, I knew the time was coming when I'd move from the U of A Hospital to the Glenrose, the same facility where I'd recovered from my ankle injury. It was a big step, because it represented the transition from acute care to rehabilitation. The Glenrose was where I'd regain my independence. I still had trouble believing that would ever happen; I still couldn't move a muscle. But at least I was covered in real skin again. And I was no longer dangerously depressed. I got frustrated and angry sometimes, and often I was too tired to be friendly or upbeat, but I no longer thought about suicide. I was ready to try.

I got a visit from a man and woman who introduced themselves as Dr. Montgomery and Caitlin, a physiatrist and an occupational therapist from the Glenrose. They were there to assess me, to see if I was ready for the move. I could see immediately that Dr. Montgomery was a happy, joyous man. His face was lit up with a smile, and I knew there was nothing to fear; I could see it in his face, his posture, and his manner. It wouldn't surprise me, during my stay at the Glenrose, when he brought me a tee-shirt from his vacation to Mexico; he thought about his patients even during his time off. That first time we met, Dr. Montgomery said my wounds needed to heal more before

I was ready for rehab, and I also had to gain a certain level of independence. Specifically, I had to be able to sit in a wheelchair.

I was determined to accomplish this feat, and to move on, and the U of A staff were determined to get me there. My sole focus became getting from the bed into the chair that sat three feet away. The whole process required four or five nurses; they pulled me into a seated position on the edge of the bed, then stood me on my feet for the time it took to turn and sit in the chair. The first time we tried it, I stretched one knee painfully far. I was out of bed for about fifteen minutes, and on my own feet for about two minutes. It felt like I was standing on razor blades, because the bottoms of my feet had been harvested for so many grafts, and that pain I experienced in my knee from bending it slightly was even worse and a prelude of things to come.

An ophthalmologist came to check my eyes and told me, "You have scar tissue a few millimetres below your pupil, and you'll always need sunglasses outside, but your vision is the same as it always was."

I thought it was a miracle.

"With all that fluid inside them, I'd have thought eyeballs would just pop in that heat," was how my dad put it.

The ophthalmologist explained how the body's reflexes to protect the eyes make them the last body part injured in any fire.

"Aren't you going to test my hearing?" I said to Dr. P.

"Can you hear me?" was his reply.

"Yeah ..."

"Then your hearing's fine."

I also had sensation tests, and wasn't surprised to learn I'd lost touch sensation permanently in some parts of my body. When they tested my feet, they told me to close my eyes. The neurologist drew numbers on my soles, and I peeked to get some of them right, as I just couldn't bear to think I couldn't feel anything, that I really never would walk again. Honestly, though, I never felt one touch, let alone a number. Thankfully, the sensation eventually came back.

A few days later, the doctors needed to know just how badly my nerves in my lower legs were damaged, as this would affect my therapy and outlook for recovery. They sent in a neurologist accompanied by five students, to assess the damage. She took out a long needle and stuck it deep into my leg. I don't know if she thought I couldn't feel it because of all the medication I was on, or because I just didn't have feeling there, but I felt it, all right. I lay there silently, probably because that was what I was good at, as she began to instruct her students. All I could think about was that needle in my leg, causing me increasing amounts of pain. After about five minutes, when I couldn't stand it anymore, I interrupted her instruction and asked her politely if she was done with that needle and if she wouldn't mind removing it. I guess she realized my nerves weren't as damaged as she'd assumed!

My hot and cold sensation had also decreased, so I'd always have to be careful while cooking or showering. I could easily burn myself and not feel it. Nowadays, I often find minor burns or cuts on my hands, and by the time I realize it there are blood drops for me to clean up throughout the house.

Christmas came and went, and then New Year's, and then out of the blue, I was going to the Glenrose.

"We're just waiting for a room," Rudi told me.

• • •

That room opened up on January 11, 2004. Tina came to the hospital early and sat with Amber in her arms, watching my nurses prepare me for the day. Once my bandages had been changed and I was dressed, they wheeled my bed into the hallway. All the staff assembled, and they had a big cake for me. Tina handed out the cards we'd prepared, thanking each of them for their help.

I was cheerful as I said my goodbyes. I couldn't wait to get in the ambulance booked for my trip across town. I was on my way to getting better; I was on my way back to real life. I was so excited, and so was Tina. One journey had ended, and a new one was about to begin.

Throughout the ambulance ride, a paramedic sat beside me, asking questions. I realized she was just there to help me stay calm. She noticed the sun was hurting my eyes, and used her clipboard to protect them. It had been so long since I had seen the sun high in the sky that I hadn't thought to ask for my sunglasses. It was a mistake I wouldn't make again. When we arrived, and that paramedic pushed me into the Glenrose in a reclining wheelchair, I couldn't help but compare the experience with the day I arrived at the U of A Hospital. There was no panic this time, and no sheet covering me. I was awake and more or less alert, with Tina and Amber at my side.

The first person we met inside was a dark-haired man who hurried over to welcome me before we even got to the elevator. He introduced himself to Tina and me as David, a registered nurse and patient care manager for my unit. "I'm in charge of organizing your care," he explained. "Which therapists you'll see and when you see them. It's my job to make sure all your treatments complement each other."

"Great," I said. "But where do you keep the beer around here?"

As David struggled for an answer, I explained I was allowed beer at the U of A because it helped me put on weight. I thought that might win him over, since I was still emaciated. I didn't mention I'd only had beer during the Grey Cup, or that, according to Kara, any weight it gave me would sit on my belly in the form of fat.

David laughed. "I'll look into that. I think we're going to get along just fine."

I never did tell him about the whisky Marc had given me.

I was wheeled into my new room and transferred onto the bed. Sure, it was just another hospital room, but for me it was a whole new world. Within minutes, we met another nurse, who noticed I couldn't press the call button beside my bed. He rigged it up with a little block of wood so all I had to do was lean on it with my hand. Things were looking up already.

As soon as all the health professionals left, I closed my eyes.

"How are you doing?" Tina asked.

"Okay, I think."

I was still excited, but I was starting to feel a bit sick and dizzy. My body seemed strange, and I was overwhelmed with the newness of everything.

Then the door opened and a tall woman with short, black hair stood over me.

"Your vacation is over," she informed me.

I stared at her in horror and disbelief.

"I'm Maria," she said. "I'll be your nurse."

I watched with dread as Maria quickly and efficiently set up the room for the next day. She laid out bandages and dressings and put together a schedule of what I'd need, never once cracking a smile.

I couldn't have guessed what was going through her head in those moments: she had recognized my name and realized I was the same Spencer Beach who'd stayed in the Glenrose less than two years earlier when I broke my ankles. She remembered sitting at the front desk and turning to see me race by in my wheelchair. She could barely believe I was that same young, handsome guy.

After Tina and Amber left that afternoon, I started vomiting. I was sick all day and evening and into the night. The Glenrose staff were alarmed by my fragility and considered sending me back to the U of A, but they decided to wait twenty-four hours. By then, I was more settled. I did, however, refuse to leave my room, and insisted that my therapists come to me. I wasn't ready to let people see me, and I don't think I was ready to see the world with everyday people yet. I hadn't realized how terrifying it would be to leave my comfort zone. Everything and everyone familiar was gone, and I had to adjust to a whole new scenario. I found I had to readjust to myself, as well. Somehow, the new surroundings emphasized how much my body had changed. Nothing around me was familiar, and I couldn't even find anything familiar about myself. All I knew was I looked like a grotesque stranger, and I couldn't move. I was helpless, insecure, lost, and institutionalized.

For two weeks, nurses brought me breakfast, lunch, and dinner in my room, and they didn't pressure me to leave, despite the general rule that patients ate together in the dining area and did their therapy downstairs, where all the equipment was.

I had two physical therapists, Linda and Kaysry, who both worked with the same assistant, Penny. Linda was the most experienced, and she took charge. She took no nonsense: she set goals and consistently moved me ahead.

The first time we met, she said, "I can't believe they sent you to us in this shape."

"I can't move at all," I acknowledged.

"Well," she said, "that's about to change."

For the first two weeks, physio was mostly concerned with stretching and rebuilding my stomach muscles. Every day, Linda asked me to roll over, and after letting me strain for a few minutes, she rolled me herself, forcing my muscles to work.

"You'll get there," she told me. "You'll be back on your feet." Just as Sharon had, she kept insisting I'd walk and run and learn to care for myself again. "My job is to eventually do nothing," she liked to tell me. "You're here to get better." She reminded me that rolling over wasn't just an exercise. It was the first step toward independence. "You'll be able to do everything you want," she said. "You just might not be able to do it the way you did before."

Then one morning, Linda placed my right leg over my left to give me a head start. I rocked back and forth three times, gaining momentum, and then I found myself lying on my left side!

"I did it!"

"Great!" said Linda. "Let's try the other side."

I couldn't quite manage rolling to the right, but within a few days, I was doing that, too. Rolling over may seem like a small feat, but it was the first sign of progress. I was no longer 100 percent helpless. Rolling over broke the false shadow of belief I had formed that I was to be bedridden for the rest of my life. I didn't just roll over that day; I also realized that I could do more if I tried. Hell, I could probably roll right out of that hospital. I was so excited. I couldn't wait for Tina to come that evening so I could show her.

I was so eager to do more that I said, "Let's go down to the therapy room." I was ready to take full advantage of the facilities.

As promised, they had special beds, called plinths, for stretching, and weights and other equipment. An occupational therapy assistant put rubber around my chair's wheels so I could, in theory, grab them, but someone, usually Kaysry, still needed to get me into the wheelchair every day and take me downstairs. That's when my recovery began in earnest, and that's when I started to feel pain like I'd never felt before.

• • •

Pain

Every injury hurts, but within a short time the victim is at the hospital, medicated to manage the pain. In rehab, real agony begins. The medication has to stop sooner or later, and rehab requires working through the pain in order to make gains back to independence.

My life fell into a predictable, if not relaxing, routine. I was in a rehab program called "intense therapy." Most patients had one or two hours of rehab a day, but for me it was an all-day event, from the moment I woke up till four in the afternoon, and each day was full of pain and more pain, topped off with an extra dose of pain. Every weekday morning, I was unceremoniously dragged from the most peaceful part of my day, the moments between sleep and wakefulness, when I didn't quite remember yet where I was, or what I had to face. Once I was awake, I needed analgesics immediately. After those came my dreaded shower. I couldn't sit up for the first while, so Maria and three other nurses moved me to the shower stretcher. They washed me all over with a special solution, removed my bandages and cleaned out all my wounds. I cried during each shower because the sensations of the water falling on me and of the bandages coming off were unbearable.

Maria shaved my head weekly, and it was so painful that I needed an extra dose of morphine with breakfast, to prepare. As far as I could tell, it never helped. "Hair holds bacteria," she explained. "I'm sorry, Spencer, but it has to come off."

Maria wheeled my shower bed into the stall, and as she glided the razor over the large, raw areas on my scalp, I pleaded with her to stop. Of course, she had to keep going. Once I was well enough to sit on a shower chair, I held a washcloth to my forehead to stop the blood from running into my face, but the shower couldn't wash that blood away before I saw it pool around my feet.

They dried me and dressed my wounds, which often took over an hour. Maria set up the meal tray and fed me, and then dressed me. Then an occupational therapy assistant came to stretch my upper body. Every joint, one at a time. Fingers, wrists, elbows, shoulders, and neck. He would say, "Tell me when it hurts," which was unnecessary, since I cringed and even screamed in pain. He pushed a little further, ripping through all the scar tissue that had developed on my ligaments and tendons. My elbows had developed a common ailment called hypertrophic ossification, which is a fancy way of saying that extra bone had grown in my elbows because they were immobile for so long. When my elbows were stretched, not only did I feel the scar tissue on my ligaments and tendons ripping apart, but the horrible sensation of bone grinding on bone. Then the porters came to help me into the wheelchair so I could go down to therapy.

My relationship with Maria changed slowly. We became friends during those mornings, mostly because my bandage changes took so long. She had to feed me in the beginning, too, because, since I still couldn't reach my mouth, feeding myself was slow and would have used up valuable therapy time. So Maria and I spent a good hour and a half together, five days a week. She told me about her family, and I told her about mine. We talked about our favourite TV shows. I even gave her advice about some of the men her daughter was dating.

I came to understand that she'd needed to take charge on that first day, when she scared me so much. I needed that good cop, bad cop dynamic; I needed someone who'd be tough, and someone else to give me tenderness, and it had to be consistent. Maria was the bad cop, and many of my therapists played good cop. I was lucky to have enough tough personalities like Maria and Linda to keep me focused, because I lost focus easily. The pain was so intense, and healing took so much energy. I was exhausted from the moment I woke up, but when I went to bed, I couldn't sleep. I took sleeping pills at around nine-thirty and turned off the TV at eleven or twelve, but I was still in so much pain from the day of therapy, it took a long time to drift off.

I usually had two physical therapy sessions each day—one with Kaysry in the morning and one with Linda after lunch. Penny was always with both of them and didn't let me get away with playing Kaysry and Linda off of each other.

Two occupational therapists, Caitlin and Darcy, worked with me for two hours after lunch. The method they used on my hands was called "serial casting," which meant they removed the casts from my hands every twenty-four hours, stretched my fingers, and then re-casted so my ligaments were permanently stretched over the whole day. My fingers were casted in a bent position, to counteract the swan-neck deformity, a distortion caused by the effect of the fire on tendons and ligaments. With a swan-neck deformity, the middle joint of the finger hyperextends and the tip of the finger is stuck in a bent position. Bending my fingers with splints and casts meant I could pick up things, and after the first day of casting, my thumbs could rotate into my palms, which greatly increased my hand function.

I couldn't lift my arms over my head, touch my face, or make a fist. Slow, steady work would increase my range of movement. To help my range of motion when I slept, as Diana and Sharon had at U of A, Caitlin and Darcy had fitted me with devices for my ankles and shoulders, and put wedges under my arms to prevent tightening under my armpits. I still had no pillow.

As I became more mobile, Caitlin and Darcy worked with me on dressing myself, bathing, and toileting. I did up buttons, played with Lego, and used my fingers to pick up things. I had to stretch my arms above my head to reach and grab things. I practised turning knobs. I could finally feed myself with ordinary cutlery, and eventually I got to practise cooking; there was a special kitchen for that purpose. We went through every activity and challenge a kitchen might pose, and they suggested ways I could adapt my surroundings and myself; for instance, they showed me a special piece of rubber I could use to open jars.

An occupational therapy assistant, Sam, often came to help me stretch, too. I knew I was the first major burn patient she'd treated, so I decided to tease her a bit. The first time I met Sam, she came into my room and stood over me, hesitating. My eyelids still didn't close completely, so when I was asleep or relaxed, my eyes rolled back in my head. I rolled my eyes forward and saw her standing there. I summoned the creepiest voice I could manage. "Call code blue," I rasped. Code blue indicates a patient requires immediate resuscitation.

"Are you serious?" she responded.

I had to laugh, and she laughed, too, probably out of relief. She proceeded to stretch and help cast my hands, and the next day, Caitlin and Darcy discovered one of my thumbs was dislocated. I hadn't even felt it.

My dealings with Sam went uphill after that, and we often laughed about the time she accidentally overstretched my thumb. It really wasn't her fault, though, as my tendons were so tight they were already applying pressure on the joint, making it vulnerable to being dislocated. Nonetheless, I liked to bug her about it. Her job consisted largely of sewing my compression garments—skin-tight sleeves for all my body parts, made to fit me exactly—and supervising me during my occupational therapy exercises. "When the scar is still red," Sam explained, "it still has an active blood supply and it can change. You have to wear the garments until the scars pale and mature, otherwise they'll grow raised and bumpy."

For my face, there was a transparent plastic mask. All those garments are notoriously itchy and uncomfortable, and I had to wear them twenty-four hours a day, except of course while bathing.

Sam put Velcro on my running shoes so I wouldn't have to tie them, and she introduced me to recreational therapy. I spent a lot of time painting and doing other art to improve my dexterity. They even brought in a lady to teach me how to paint by blowing through a straw at paint on a canvas. I made paintings for everyone.

Every afternoon, Linda and Penny stretched my lower body. I often screamed as Linda stretched my hips, knees, and ankles. Kaysry explained that they were actually creating "micro tears" in the tissue so it would gradually stretch and become more mobile. It's impossible to describe how painful that was. I dreaded therapy, and I wasted a lot of breath trying to talk them out of doing it. Even my usual cocktail of methadone, morphine, and Tylenol 3, and dreams of a future when I could walk and take care of myself, couldn't eliminate the agony. Then, after dinner, my bandages had to be changed again, by the evening nurse.

My progress at the Glenrose was relentless and amazing. Within months, Caitlin and Darcy had me feeding myself and brushing my own teeth. And the more I healed, the more time I had to look in the mirror that occupied the usual space above my sink. As I started brushing my own teeth, I had to spend those minutes confronted by my new face. I avoided looking at myself too closely, but I knew I'd have to deal with the truth sooner or later. Sam told me the story she'd heard of a female burn patient who avoided looking in the mirror at all until she got home, and then had a severe emotional breakdown.

Linda, Kaysry, and Penny got my body moving to the point where they could pull me into a sitting position and then a standing one. It took half an hour to get me on the tilt table, which is used to tilt a patient into a standing position. Since I was so tall, and couldn't bend my knees, it took several people to hoist me to my feet without the tilt table. But I was standing for minutes at a time, I could sit in the shower instead of lying, and I could help wash myself. There were still plenty of challenges to face. One of the worst was that my hands and feet became hypersensitive, a temporary condition that meant the slightest touch sent pain rippling through my body.

"It's like a fireworks show," was how I described it. "That little ball of light launched in the air is you touching me, and what I feel is the massive explosion going out in all directions."

All evening, my legs pulsated. The pain began in my knees and vibrated down each leg, through my feet, and out my toes. There was no position that eased the pain; the only thing that helped was Ativan, and I didn't get that until nine-thirty. Then, all night, I suffered arthritic pain in my ankles.

But things were getting better, just like the therapists had promised. I could stand, though only for a minute because of the pain in my feet; I could bear wearing shoes for five minutes, and then I needed a break. Linda said my ankles were just too weak to support me, with the bone damage from my previous accident compounded by nerve and muscle damage from the fire. She had me fit with ankle-foot orthotics—AFOs. The plastic splints wrapped under my feet and went up to the base of each knee. The AFOs did stop my ankles from buckling, but they made standing even more painful, because now I was standing on hard plastic. Linda tried to pad them, but nothing really helped.

I couldn't balance, so the therapists hovered around me as I stood, and I had a special belt around my waist in case they needed to catch me. I gradually developed my equilibrium. The next exercise was to get on my feet by myself, which was hard because my knees wouldn't bend fully. I worked on standing on one foot. Soon it would be time to try walking.

• • •

And I was beginning to deal with a different kind of agony, too. Down in the therapy room, I was in the midst of many patients with therapists and visitors. Linda had talked to me about the inevitable stares I'd get, and asked me how I planned to deal with the attention.

"I don't care," I said. "I'm still who I am."

I tried to ignore the looks, but they bothered me more than I'd anticipated. I realized I needed another kind of help—help coming to terms with being a burn guy, out in public. That public was only going to grow, and my disfigurement would never go away.

During the first two weeks, when I was holed up in my room, a woman around my parents' age had come to see me. Unlike everyone else, she was wearing a blouse and trousers instead of scrubs. She introduced herself as Dr. Mann and said she was a psychologist who worked with burn patients and people living with chronic illnesses.

"I see people down in my office," she told me. "When you're ready, come down, and we'll talk."

We spoke for a few minutes, and throughout the next two weeks I thought about what she told me. She said I'd been working hard to survive, and that I'd still be working hard with all my therapists, nurses, and doctors on getting my body working again. "You're already rebuilding the outside," she said. "But I look at the inside of the house."

Dr. Mann was by no means the first psychologist who'd spoken to me, nor was she the first person to mention the emotional hurdles I'd have to face along with my physical ordeals. But I could tell right away there was something different about her. Every counsellor, psychologist, and psychiatrist listens, but Dr. Mann listened and cared, and she responded in a way I could understand. She seemed to have no biases. I must have been among the strangest-looking people she'd ever met, but she treated me as though I were normal. I knew it was no act: it was who she was. She saw through my burnt-out exterior—that unkempt yard with its broken fence boards and weeds—and took the time to find the clear spots in my windows. She saw, as she said, into the inside of the house.

Shortly after I started leaving my room, I asked to see Dr. Mann. It was one of the best decisions I ever made. Throughout my therapy with her, which continued even after I left the hospital, Dr. Mann was a precious jewel in my life. For reasons I can't quite explain, I trusted her completely. I knew if I were open and honest with her, she would help me. She, in turn, understood that I wanted to meet my demons head-on, and she was always straightforward with me. If I asked her a question, she answered it. If I sought criticism or advice, she told me straight up what she thought. She knew how to draw pictures so I could understand what she meant.

Dr. Mann kept pointing out how I put other people's needs above my own, how I wanted to provide for and protect my loved ones, even if that meant disregarding my own needs.

"I don't mind being hurt," I told Dr. Mann. "I can handle it. I just don't want to be a burden on Tina. I can't stand hurting her."

"You need to be strong."

"I am strong," I said. "I'm still the same person on the inside. I just have a new package. And that package is weak right now, but it'll get strong again, too."

"That's true," said Dr. Mann. She had a soft voice and a way of rocking in her chair when she spoke. Just watching her and listening to her was soothing. "You have tremendous strength and courage and positivity. You're a compassionate, sensitive person. But do you know what's on the other side of that coin?"

"What?"

"Vulnerability. You're sensitive to other people's feelings. And you've been through a terrible trauma, Spencer. You're going through hell. Those things make you vulnerable."

"I'm not vulnerable," I insisted.

Dr. Mann often went back to this theme, in her gentle way, telling me that my vulnerability was not a weakness but a strength.

Most of the Glenrose staff—and most of the people who knew me—would describe me as upbeat and positive. I always made an effort to be pleasant with the other patients, and I developed quite a reputation in the hospital. As Linda once said, I wasn't known as "Spencer the burn patient," but as "Spencer the talkative, friendly burn patient."

But with Dr. Mann, I showed the other side of the coin. The side where my fears and insecurities lay. The side that held my frustration over having "burn patient" included in any possible description of me, and over the fact that I'd have to deal with that identifier for the rest of my life. Some days I'd arrive in her office joking with the attendant pushing my chair, but would find myself in tears a few minutes later, asking Dr. Mann, "Why would anyone want to be my friend?"

When Linda stretched my limbs each day, I saw how scarred they were, and how painfully thin. I spent two hours each day watching my deformed hands as my occupational therapists tried to convince what was left of my fingers to bend forward instead of backward. I knew what I looked like, even if I wasn't facing it head-on yet, and I couldn't imagine anyone choosing to spend time with me. In the hospital, people were paid to care for me and treat me with compassion. My family and friends felt too sorry for me to turn away. I knew I was living in a bubble.

And it was troubling in another way, too. I used to joke with my female nurses and doctors that it wasn't fair how they got to see me naked all the time and I never got to see them naked. After all, my naked body was quite a unique specimen. It was true emotionally as well as physically that I was always exposed to people who didn't let me see anything of them. My nurses and therapists knew everything about me, but when I asked questions about their lives, they laughed at best and reprimanded me at worst. They always reminded me to respect "boundaries." They were health professionals, in other words, and I was a patient, and as intimate as our contact might seem, we could never really be friends.

What would happen when I got out in the real world? Would I maintain and create real, genuine friendships? How could anyone ever get over the scars? I told Dr. Mann what I used to be like. How good looking, confident, and macho I was. I didn't know how to be in the world without that persona. Would I ever be anything beyond a misfit, a freak—a burn guy? I couldn't imagine why Tina, or any woman, would choose me when there were millions of men whose bodies weren't riddled with scars, who had noses and ears, who wouldn't attract the eyes of everyone they passed.

Dr. Mann listened to me and supported me. She also gave me practical suggestions for easing into public life with trips to places I felt comfortable, when I was ready. Thank God I had her to talk with as I steeled myself for whatever "real life" as a burn guy would turn out to be. My occupational therapists gave me some good advice, too. They suggested smiling at people I caught checking me out, so they would realize there was an ordinary man behind my scars. They also suggested I come up with a generic answer for curious strangers asking me what had happened. I couldn't have anticipated how often that would happen! It's amazing how many strangers feel comfortable asking me personal questions. Luckily, I'm not a private or reserved person.

Sometimes I was too sad to talk much during my sessions with Dr. Mann, and she let me sit in silence. She helped me understand that I was grieving, which is different from being depressed. I was depressed at the U of A Hospital, but I'd pulled myself out of it. With grief, sadness comes and goes.

"Will I ever get over this?" I asked her.

"I don't think one ever gets over trauma, exactly," she said after considering my question. "But you'll find harmony with it."

The most powerful words Dr. Mann ever said to me were simply, "You're not crazy." Those words are still a source of confidence when I find the reality of my burns hard to handle. I remind myself that I'm not crazy, or burned; I am an extremely hot man.

• • •

I drove all my therapists a bit nuts, because I insisted on knowing why they did everything, and how it worked. I often suggested they splint my hands a different way, or stretch me differently, and I didn't give in to their methods until they convinced me with solid facts and evidence that I was wrong and they were right. When Linda told me I was standing up wrong, pushing off with my knees instead of transferring my weight over my feet, I wouldn't believe her.

I argued so much, she finally said, "Okay, that's fine. I can just go home. If you want to stay at this level, that's your problem."

When she calmed her temper, she had a series of people stand and made me watch how their bodies moved. She was right.

Although my therapists rolled their eyes at my constant questioning, they also told me they were impressed because I was engaged in my treatment and took initiative. I happily did my stretches alone on the weekends, as instructed, and all my therapists were glad I wasn't passive. I wasn't one of those patients who'd stop exercising as soon as I was discharged, to spend the rest of my life in an armchair in front of the TV. There was no way that was happening to me.

I was so active in my care that I was eventually invited to take part in a study group to improve patient care. That process began thanks to David, the patient care manager I met on my first day, who often came to make sure I was getting what I needed and that care on the unit complemented my therapy. We got to know each other well. He always asked me how I was doing, and one day I said, "You know what drives me really nuts?"

"What?" he asked, sitting down beside my bed.

"Well, you know that time in the morning when you're coming out of sleep but haven't completely woken up? That's the one time in a twenty-four-hour period when I'm not in pain. I don't remember where I am yet, and I'm my old self. It's the best part of my day. But then these damn nurses come in, turn on all the lights, and wake me up in two seconds! They're not gentle about it either. It's *Wake up right now and start your day*."

David listened to me thoughtfully. He said he knew what I meant, that nursing staff become immune to the devastating things that have happened to people, and just want to get efficiently through their days, according to their schedules. "I struggled with that, too, when I was a nurse," David admitted. Then he explained the concept of "people-centred care," which he said was a major movement in hospitals across Canada. He said the Glenrose was trying to be there for the patients, without just fitting them into blocks of time, and that from what I'd said he knew they had a lot of work to do. "It's a monstrous shift," he said, describing how many hospitals were including patients in their committees and in all major decisions. He suggested that when I was well enough, I should take on some of those responsibilities. I ended up doing just that, and David told me I'd helped his staff become better nurses.

• • •

One of the best things about my time in the Glenrose was the weight it took off my family. Until I left the U of A Hospital, they were still afraid I might die. Now I was officially on the mend. I got more visitors than before, and I received them with more grace. Grandpa Beach came at least once a week; he always came unannounced during the day. I know Grandma Jekabson wanted to come that often, too, but it was hard for her to get a ride from the other side of town. She came when she could.

My mother visited me every night, and my parents often cooked me dinner to help me regain weight, because let's face it, hospital food sucks, especially after eating it every day for over a year. One night, Grant took me out for dinner right there in my room. He brought my favourites: steak and coconut shrimp from Outback, a chain restaurant. And of course Tina still came every day.

On my thirtieth birthday, Tina threw a surprise party in my room. She and Amber were there, along with my whole family and most of my friends. Even Sharon from the U of A Hospital dropped by. We ate an ice cream cake from Dairy Queen, and that was the most cheerful I'd felt since the fire.

At one point, Vail confided in me how much the fire had shaken him and all of Jack's workers. "We thought we were being careful," he said, "just opening the windows and turning down the furnace. I guess we were all ignorant of the danger of what we were doing. We'd all done the same kind of thing." I realized what all the guys on my crew must have been thinking—that it could just as easily have been them. I also realized that, then, when the boss has a joke "K-BOOM" licence plate made up to commemorate an accident, safety becomes just that to the workers. A joke.

Because of what happened to me, Vail and the other workers would never again use a chemical without reading up on it first. They would insist on safety instruction, and when they received it, they would take it seriously. What if there was some way I could tell more people about my accident? People who worked in dangerous trades and didn't take safety seriously, because they were too intent on getting their work done and making money? Because they were too tough? Dr. Mann said talking to people about the accident was the best thing I could do; it was a positive way of releasing my anger. When I got out of the hospital and regained enough mobility and confidence, I decided, I was going to spread the word about safety.

When I told my mother about my plan, she was supportive, but I knew she must have had trouble picturing me out in the world pursuing a career, especially one that involved roomfuls of people staring at me. She and Tina and my other loved ones were glad I was determined to do something with the rest of my life, but I'm not sure how seriously they took my dreams of advocacy. Not that they didn't think I was capable. They were just too focused on my learning simple tasks like standing and putting on my socks.

• • •

And then at last it was time to try walking. Linda scheduled me in to use the parallel bars, and I told Tina and my father. Dad had told me he wanted to be there, and he was happy to hold Amber so Tina could give me her full attention.

Linda secured a special tray to the parallel bars because my hands prevented me from gripping the bars like most patients would do. When the time came, I stood up from the chair, put my arms on the tray so it supported my weight, and took a step. And another. Linda followed me the whole way with my wheelchair. She didn't expect me to walk the whole length, but slowly, painfully, step after step, I made it.

As I sat down, she turned me around and said, "We're done."

"No," I told her. "I didn't come all the way down here just to walk thirty feet. I'm going to do it again."

Linda set me up and I walked back the other way, slower this time. I made it almost halfway.

"Okay," I said. "Now I'm done."

I let Linda help me into the wheelchair.

That's when I noticed Tina and my dad both had tears in their eyes. My father says he knew that day I wasn't going to let this thing beat me.

I was going to work so hard, like he had come to expect from me at Beach Brothers, that I'd inspire my doctors and therapists. I'd show them new levels of what a burn patient could achieve. There was no doubt in my mind.

• • •

Tough

I tell my audiences I can sum up the mistakes that led to my injury—that lead to most workplace accidents—in a simple saying, one that everyone in the trades has heard before, probably on a daily basis. That saying is, "Get it done."

When I worked for Jack, I wanted to do my job properly, and to me that meant working hard, working fast, not complaining, and not questioning anything my employer said. When Jack told me something needed to happen, I got it done. Safety was not a concern for him and wasn't a concern for me, either. Generations of workers, even in my own family, have needlessly risked their health and lives because of that mentality. Countless people have lost children, parents, friends, and spouses. Why? Because we're tough. By that, I mean we think we're invincible; we just want to get it done, and consider it a waste of time at best and a sign of weakness at worst to get it done *safely*. I always thought a tough man was strong, fearless, and capable—all the things I strived to be. But now I know the word's other meaning—I know that tough means *difficult*. Tough is living a life like mine.

I tell my audiences: "Working and playing safely mean that when you get to your deathbed, you can look back on your life and say, 'I had a great life. No incident ever slowed me down. No disability ever complicated my life. I did everything I ever hoped to do.' When I get to my deathbed, it will probably be premature, from complications related to my burns. I'll look back and say, 'I had a tough life. It was complicated. It was slowed down. I didn't get to do everything I ever wanted to. My injury affected everyone I cared about, and it didn't have to happen.' I'm tough. I have to live with that." Is it really tough to risk ruining the lives of everyone you love? I'll tell you what's tough. Tough is putting my face out in this world every single day.

• • •

The first time I left the Glenrose and put my new self out in that world, I went to church. It was February 2004, and I went to my daughter's baptism. Though she was born in September, we didn't baptize her until I could be there. It would be the first time since Boxing Day and my transfer to the Glenrose that I had left the hospital.

Reagan and Craig came to the hospital a few days before, and Linda explained how to transfer me. She told them they'd have to help me in the bathroom and asked them how they felt about that; she told us not to ask Tina to do those tasks. "Tina is going to have enough emotional stress," she said. "She's going to be the wife and mother, and you brothers are going to be the caregivers." Reagan and Craig were great about it. They assured Linda they were up for the challenge, and I didn't feel uncomfortable about them helping me.

But I was scared. I knew that if I'd died, I'd have watched Amber's baptism from heaven. But I didn't die, and I wasn't light as air. My body was burdensome, and getting it to that church was an ordeal that had required days of planning. I had to be transferred onto a reclining wheelchair and then driven to the church in a special taxi for people with disabilities, all with the help of attendants and my brothers. This was the first time since the fire I'd enter a roomful of people beyond immediate family, knowing they'd all turn and stare. I tried not to assume they'd be looking with suppressed horror. I knew I'd be the focal point of the room. The burn guy.

Fortunately, my fear was overshadowed by the importance of my daughter's baptism, and my determination that if I couldn't witness her birth, I must at least witness her initiation into the church. Baptism is more than a child becoming a child of God; it's also a commitment on the part of the parents, the godparents—in this case, Craig and Sandra—and the whole church family. And Dr. Mann was right: I'd have to get used to being around people eventually. This was the best way I could ease myself into that experience. I'd be among friends. I reminded myself that going to church meant being surrounded by people who cared, people who loved me. We're a hugging church. You walk in and everyone's hugging you, and you're welcome there. When everything else falls apart, that's one group that never judges. And now my daughter would be a lifelong member of that group.

Pastor Habben, of course, had known since Amber's birth how much I wanted to attend her baptism, and I understood just how welcome and safe I would feel in his church when he told me the congregation had built a ramp, just for me.

I was dressed early for the ten o'clock service, and I waited and waited, but the taxi didn't show up until 9:50. I was anxious and disappointed as they wheeled me out, sure I'd miss at least part of this important day; but when we arrived at the church, I discovered the congregation had prayed so much for me, and had anticipated her baptism so much, they'd postponed the service and waited for me.

Despite all my fear, and all the eyes on me, I was comfortable. The baptismal font in our church is made of concrete to symbolize the rock, which is the word of God. Sandra held Amber, because she was the godmother, and the congregation vowed to support our daughter in her spiritual needs. Pastor Habben drew crosses with holy water on Amber's heart, her forehead, and her body and then baptized her with handfuls of holy water on her head, three times.

Some of the congregation had already seen me in the hospital, and after the baptism, everyone came over to say hello. They said they were glad to have me back, and I knew they meant it. "What blessings you have," they told me.

After church, we went to my parents' house for a party, and after a couple of hours, the special taxi came back and took me to the Glenrose. It was a stressful but truly awesome day.

• • •

After Amber's baptism, I started getting regular evening passes. I usually went home in a taxi on Monday and Tuesday evenings, stayed for the night, and went back to the hospital in the morning. I always looked forward to those evenings at home; they meant I was on my way back into a regular life; they meant relaxing with my wife and daughter instead of languishing in the boredom of hospital life. They meant Tina didn't have to visit me; I could visit her instead. But they also meant realizing just what a burden I was on her. I had to relearn every aspect of functioning inside my home; that was the point of those passes, to readjust to the realities of regular life and to solve the problems I might encounter while we still had the hospital to help me.

At that time, Tina and I were barely a couple, although we were happy to be back together. Instead, we had more of a caregiver-patient relationship. During my time in the hospital, so much had changed. Tina was a mother now, and she had her own routines and responsibilities. It was horrible to realize that instead of relieving some of Tina's stress, I was another baby she had to care for. I stayed in my own separate bedroom downstairs so I wouldn't disturb her each evening when the home-care nurses came to put me to bed, and so I wouldn't wake Tina and Amber when the home-care nurses came to help me get ready and then take me back to the Glenrose in the mornings.

Linda and Caitlin had assessed my home and rearranged my kitchen so it would work for me. Since we had a glass table and no arms on the kitchen chairs, they suggested I eat at the counter. They provided a rail for my bed and one for the toilet to help me get up and down, and they installed a chair in my shower. Caitlin suggested handles in the tubs and levers instead of doorknobs, but I told her no. I didn't want my tubs and doors wrecked. I would find a way to adapt to the mechanisms in my home, and only when I couldn't find a way would anything be adapted to me.

I sure didn't choose the easy way, and inside that house, I faced an obstacle course. The house was a four-level split, with bathrooms only on the top and bottom floors. Every time I needed the bathroom, I put on my ankle-foot orthotics and made the painful and arduous climb up or down the stairs. The doors were always closed because of Amber, and though my hands were still hypersensitive, I always tried to turn the knob before I asked Tina to help me. I hated making her climb those stairs—usually with Amber in tow—just to let me into the bathroom. Finally, once I was inside, I faced the toilet. An obstacle in itself. Using an ordinary toilet was one of the many daily tasks I'd relearned with the help of my OTs. Now it was a matter of practice.

One thing I could help with was the dishes. It was relatively easy to place each plate and utensil in the dishwasher after dinner; the only problem was I couldn't open the door. After dinner, or whenever I wanted a clean glass, I'd go to that dishwasher and squeeze the release as hard as I could. Though pain would rip through my fingers, the lever wouldn't budge. Eventually, I became so frustrated that I just stopped trying. "Tina," I'd say. "Can you open this for me?"

"Did you try?"

"No."

"Well, try," she told me.

I grabbed the handle and wrestled with it for a few seconds. "There. I can't open it!"

Tina was patient, but she never let me get away with not trying. And then one day as I pressed and squeezed, proving to her I couldn't do it, the release clicked, and the door eased open.

I started getting weekend passes from Friday night until Monday morning. Weekends were the most boring time at the hospital, and now I could spend them with my family. And I could go to church. Although Tina was never religious, she came with me every Sunday, and spending that time with my wife and baby made me try harder during the week, when I was back at the hospital. I couldn't be discharged until I was deemed safe to take care of myself and to get around town to my ongoing therapy sessions.

• • •

Before I could go home for good, I also had to stop taking the drugs I'd become addicted to. I was used to taking methadone twice a day, so I was under its effects all the time. I took morphine for extreme pain, and I was allowed Tylenol 3 between the morphine doses. All the drugs were extremely addictive, and I was far more addicted to all of them than I'd ever been to cocaine or pot. Of course, that was partly because without methadone, morphine, and Tylenol 3, I quickly found myself in pain. I believe it was mostly the pain, not the addiction, that brought me back to those medications after trying several times to cut them out of my routine.

Dr. Montgomery finally weaned me off methadone by gradually decreasing the doses until one day he told me I was taking a placebo. The doctors had warned my parents that severly injured people often end up addicted to drugs and alcohol for the rest of their lives, using painkillers to numb their grief and anger. My mother was a little worried about that and probably would have been more worried if I hadn't hidden my former fondness for drugs so well. Her concern eased when she saw how determined I was to leave the hospital addiction free, and to stay that way. And I have.

During my hospital stay, I had gone through withdrawal from tobacco and marijuana without even noticing it. I remember how pot was once such a huge part of my identity. I smoked it every day until my accident, but I have barely touched it since. My friends have learned not to offer me drugs anymore, because I'll say no. I don't have anything against pot in general; I believe there's a time and place for everything, and I just can't seem to find the time or place for pot anymore. Unlike before, I don't believe it has any place in a workday, in the context of motor vehicles, or around open flames like campfires, when the closest hospital is miles away. The only vice I still succumb to sometimes is cigarettes. That really makes Reagan and Kelly crazy, because of the fire's damage to my lungs.

After I stopped taking painkillers, it hurt more than ever to walk, and I still had some hypersensitivity in my hands. Gripping a handle hurt, but I did it anyway, and I still couldn't turn over the key in a car. Otherwise, I was already pain free. My skin didn't hurt; my lungs didn't hurt; my joints didn't hurt except when stretched. It will probably surprise many readers to learn that burn survivors don't generally suffer from chronic pain. Once burns heal, they look far worse than they feel. Once a burn survivor adapts to any ensuing disabilities, disfigurement is his heaviest cross to bear. That's why it's so easy for me to forget I'm a burn guy until I notice the stares or catch a glimpse of my reflection. Then I remind myself that they stare because I am so damn hot.

• • •

At the Glenrose, every patient's room had a little white board with a discharge date. Throughout my stay, my board had been blank, but in my mind, April 24 was the day I was leaving. I was determined to go home a year after my accident.

When that day came, Linda told me, "We know you want to go home today, but we all think you'd benefit from another couple of months."

The Workers' Compensation Board would send me for daily rehab at the Millard Health Centre after I was discharged, and I'd still return to the Glenrose for some treatment, but I wouldn't get as much individual attention. Linda said I wasn't quite ready to be so self-directed.

"It's up to you," she said. But I knew I didn't really have a choice. I would be crazy to ignore her. I nodded my consent.

"Okay, Spencer," she said. "Two months."

When Tina came in that day, I had to tell her I was staying. But I also showed her my white board, with my discharge date written across it in bold letters: June 24. The end was in sight. And I was spending more and more time at home already. I think she was happy with how the Glenrose handled this situation and with my decision to tough it out.

Those two months passed quickly, and I worked harder than ever with my PTs and OTs. Linda upped the ante in our therapy. One day she put her face above me and told me to punch her, so I'd stretch my arm. The next day, she came in with a helmet. She even brought in her young daughters and had them kick soccer balls at me so I could play goalie. We worked on deep breathing, posture, endurance, stairs, and function. I was game for everything.

On June 24, I was assessed and deemed fit for discharge. At lunchtime, I went to my room, where Tina and Amber were waiting for me. Tina helped me put on jeans because I wanted to wear them for the first time since the accident. I wanted to leave that hospital feeling normal, not wearing track pants because they were functional. This just revealed one more challenge I would have to overcome. Buttons. We went down to the party. Everyone hugged me and said goodbye. And most of them said, "Oh my gosh! You're wearing jeans!"

We had cake and pizza, and they made me cut the cake. I handed out at least twenty cards for my doctors, nurses, and therapists. Tina and I had picked them out together, and each card was unique. The most amazing part was, I wrote in each one myself.

Then we went to my room and packed. We put most of my bags in the baby carriage, and I pushed it down to the parking lot. Walking down that hallway for the last time, I took my time. I thought about the day I came in, immobile in a reclining wheelchair, and relished how far I'd come. I came to that hospital as helpless as a baby and five months later, I walked out pushing a baby stroller, with my wife beside me. I was going home to be a father, a husband, a man, and a normal person. A person who makes mistakes and learns from them.

Tina had placed a big "Welcome Home" sign in the window at home and had prepared a little celebration for me. I don't even remember what we did that night. We just relaxed. We began to be a family again. The transition from the hospital back home was exactly that. A transition. But I was home. I had a two-week break from therapy so I could have some time for myself, and during that break, we didn't do much. We just took it easy and started getting back to living.

• • •

Then I started therapy at the Millard Centre, which would be my home away from home for the next few years. I started working with Dave, their physical therapist, toward walking unaided and eventually running, achieving better balance, squatting and kneeling—necessary for many tasks, but especially important for the parent of a toddler. Dave was a great guy, but when I suggested we go out for a beer, he said he wasn't allowed to fraternize with his clients.

"You can never meet me for a drink?"

"I can have a beer with you in seven years," he said.

"It's a date." After that, I kept a running countdown, to make him laugh. "Only three more years till that beer, buddy!" I called across the room when I saw him recently.

When I started at the Millard, my main home-care nurse was a pretty girl called Carrie. She had some strict rules, like she could see me naked but I couldn't see her. Every nurse had that rule! Every morning, she helped me into the shower. I sat on my chair, and she was supposed to wash me down. "No way," I told her. "I've got to do things myself. What am I supposed to do when you're not here?"

After I showered, Carrie wrapped a towel around my shoulders and helped me with my AFOs. I walked back to my room and took the braces back off, and Carrie put on my few remaining bandages and helped me with my compression garments. I could manage my street clothes myself, though the first time I dressed myself took forty-seven minutes and I needed help with my socks.

One morning, after a few months at the Millard, I got out of the shower and said to Carrie, "Please get my walker. I want to try walking without the braces."

"Not without a therapist's recommendation," she said.

But I could be pretty convincing. "I know my limitations. I'm not putting myself in danger. You won't get in trouble," I said. "I promise."

Carrie walked beside me as I put my weight on the walker and slowly made my way from the bathroom back to my bed. After that day, she let me walk each morning with the walker and no braces. I didn't tell anyone. It was our secret. I also found out why a penis is called a ding-dong as it swung back and forth.

Then one morning, I said, "Let's try it without the walker."

"No way, Spence," Carrie said.

"Come on. Just a couple of steps. We'll keep the walker right here in case I need it. And you're here, too."

Of course, I was buck-naked at this point. Maybe that's why she gave in. The longer we argued, the longer I'd stay nude. She did let me take a few steps, and I stayed upright, though my left ankle kept trying to buckle. Then Carrie, probably seeing her career pass before her eyes, pushed the walker into my hands.

That day at the Millard, I asked Dave if I could practise without my braces.

"Okay," he said. "But you need a cane."

And I walked with the cane the whole length of the therapy room.

Dave, of course, didn't know about my secret morning walks. He looked impressed and a little surprised. "Start with the cane inside your house," he advised. "I think you should still use the braces for a while when you're out. I know this is a big step for you, but your ankles need time to get used to it."

That day, I cried for the first time in a long while. Those braces were such a trap, such a limitation to me. Without them, I had no more aids. I didn't need assistance; I didn't need anything. I was myself again. I was a burnt version of me, but that seemed a small concession. I decided to keep my ankle-foot orthotics forever, to remind me of how precious my freedom was.

When I returned home that evening, I tromped through the house in my shoes, as usual; I always wore shoes in the house, because I needed them to hold my braces in place. Tina was out back with her friend, who also had a baby son. I let myself fall into a lawn chair, and Tina could see I'd been crying as I played it up.

"What's wrong?"

"I had a crappy day!"

"What happened?"

I took off my braces and threw them across the yard.

"Spence, what happened?"

I stood up and walked over to her. It took Tina a minute to notice I wasn't wearing my braces. She was so proud of me. I cried again while she hugged me.

After that, I only wore the AFOs if I was going out to the mall or another place where I'd have to walk for a long time. My ankles strengthened quickly.

Dave soon had me packing weight in a backpack and walking up and down the Millard Centre stairs. I did balance-beam work, I did lunges and squats between the parallel bars, and Dave showed me how to sit on the floor and get back up, using the wall for support. Therapists love to demonstrate how to do things, so you can see the correct body dynamics, and that works great for me, because I'm a very visual person. It was hard at first, but once I did it, I kept practising. To this day, I need to support myself with my hands when I kneel. My ankles are the weakest part of my body.

Hand therapy was more tricky. I liked my therapist, Debbie, immediately, especially how she reacted to each of my jokes and comments by saying something equally outrageous back. But there's no rule book to deal with hands as damaged as mine were; we just used reason and Debbie's knowledge. My right hand responded to her exercises and splinting, but my left hand didn't improve at all. It was just too badly damaged.

Dr. P. convinced me to get my left hand fused. I didn't want to, but he assured me the procedure would improve my life. They broke all my fingers and stuck pins through to immobilize them, and my hand was in a cast for three months, my fingers bent in a position that would let me pick things up. Eventually, my left arm became stronger than my right because the fusion allowed me to use my muscles more efficiently.

Debbie continued with splinting, casting, stretching, you name it. Nothing really worked. I gained strength and function in my right hand, but not much in ability. In other words, I learned how to do things, but I still couldn't move my fingers much. My goal with my hands was to not need any aids. I wanted to use my hands the way they were. My main motivation in all my therapy was to gain enough strength and control that I could care for my daughter. The first time Tina left Amber in my care, she was over a year old. Tina's mother came to stay the night with us just in case, for her own peace of mind. My therapists suggested I hold Amber over a table in case she slipped out of my arms. I took their advice, but there was no way I was dropping my daughter.

I regularly went to visit my old therapists at the Glenrose and filled them in on my progress. I was so excited the day I got to tell Linda I could hold Amber, and the day I told her I was changing my daughter's diapers. Each time I told Linda what I'd achieved, she suggested new goals, even though I was no longer officially in her care. "Okay, you can walk up stairs," she said. "Try running."

Linda says my gait is now so normal, she'd never be able to tell, from watching me walk, that I'd been hurt at all. From behind, if I'm wearing long pants and sleeves, and a hat, I look like a regular guy. And for a long time, I wouldn't have dreamed of leaving my house without covering every possible inch of my body. Striding confidently down a crowded sidewalk in shorts and a tee-shirt still seemed about as likely as heading out completely nude.

• • •

Burn Guy

As I regained function, I became increasingly independent, and eventually I was bathing and grooming alone, with no attendant. All that grooming meant standing at the sink, and that meant looking in the mirror for more and more time. I started to really look at my face. I remember one day, I forced myself to stand in front of the mirror and I looked long and hard. I examined my patchwork skin, my shiny scalp with its patchy hair, my red-rimmed eyes. I saw how the shape of my lower lip had distorted because of the scar tissue on my neck dragging my jawline down. I saw how the cartilage on my nose was gone. Eventually, I would have reconstructive surgery to fix that, but for now I had oversized nostrils, and the whole world could see right inside them. I had no ears. This was me. This was what I looked like now, and I was going to have to deal with it.

I phoned Marc and told him, "Dude, I did it."

To move past the burns, I had to accept the burns. I had to change the way I viewed myself to include the fire. It may seem ironic that, in order to fully heal, I had to acknowledge that I was permanently disfigured and disabled, but that understanding helped tremendously in letting go of my anger. Since then, I've met people who don't include their injury, sickness, or disability in their self-concept. Those people make decisions based not on facts, but on lies based on how they used to be. They make poor decisions trying to do things the same ways they used to, and they set themselves up for failure. Each time they fail, they become increasingly angry. I remember one day in physical therapy, I heard another client lamenting that she couldn't clean her house because of a shoulder injury. She loved her house, but was afraid she'd lose it if her shoulder didn't improve. She was miserable.

"Listen," I said. "You may never be able to clean those high shelves or mow your lawn again. Since your house means so much to you, you need to find a solution. Crying about it won't help; it'll only let your disability take more from you. Instead, you can look for ways to get those chores done, even if it means hiring someone. Find the things you can do, and accept those you can't. Otherwise you'll just hurt yourself more and you'll end up losing your house."

Injured people are truly incapacitated when they don't see themselves as disabled and try to do things the same ways they always did. That mindset causes anger, grief, disappointment, and self-hatred. Ironically, those emotions often make us more disabled, as we give up things we could do, with a little effort. Those who accept their disabilities and incorporate them into their daily lives find new, safe, and effective ways of living. Instead of disappointment over seemingly constant failure, we find joy in the things we can do. Tasks we struggle with become sources of happiness, too, as we continue to try to do them, and, more often than not, figure out ways to manage them.

Because I accepted my limitations, and their permanence, I constantly looked for new, realistic ways to adjust, to figure out the small and big things I used to do without thinking.

One day when Marc came to pick me up, I said, "You don't have to tie my shoes anymore!" I showed him how my dexterity was improving and how I could finally bend over far enough to touch my feet.

One of my greatest victories came when I passed my driver's test in an unmodified car. I didn't want my new wheels wrecked with a bunch of extra accessories, just like I didn't want my bathrooms wrecked by installing hand rails, so I taught myself how to work with what was there.

And when I looked long and hard at my new face, it started getting easier to go out in public. I started going for short walks around the block. Eventually, I tried going out for the whole day, going to restaurants and bars and even sporting events, where hundreds and thousands of strangers would see me.

The first time I'd gone out without Tina or my parents, one of my nurses at the Glenrose took me for lunch at the Royal Alexandra Hospital. We didn't have to go outside to get there, since the two hospitals are connected by a tunnel system. I was going to have a coffee. When we got to the café, all I could see were all those eyes looking at me. I got so flustered that I ordered an iced tea instead of the coffee I really wanted.

When I started venturing farther, I couldn't believe how many mirrors there were everywhere. Every time I walked past a window, I realized with a shock that the reflection looking back was me, and my heart was ripped in two. It hurt so much because seeing myself reminded me how much my mistakes had cost my family. And I knew that no matter how successful my operations were, I'd always look like I'd been through a fire. I'd always be disabled. I'd always have a body riddled with scars and I'd always have a disfigured face. Forever, every photo in my family album would feature a burn guy in the middle of it.

Back then, I was focusing on the burns, constantly seeing myself from the outside. When I met a new person, or made eye contact with a curious stranger, I thought of my burns and felt like a hopeless misfit, incapable of blending into a crowd ever again.

And to be honest, some people were mean. Sometimes teenagers or even adults called out, "Freak!" as I walked by. Strangely enough, that didn't bother me the way I thought it would. Those people just seemed sad and ignorant to me, unable to see past the surface of things, unable to exercise a little compassion, unable to see the person in that body. Too bad for them, because I am really a funny, lighthearted person.

The vast majority of the people I met were pleasant and nice. People did stare, but they treated me kindly. As always, I put others and myself at ease by joking. My first dinner out, with Tina, Amber, my father-in-law, and Marc, was a much-anticipated trip to the Keg. I was still using ankle-foot orthotics and a walker, I was wearing compression garments and bandages, and my left hand was in a cast. I could feel every eye on me.

When the waiter asked me how I wanted my steak, I said, "Not as well done as I am, please."

He was too shocked to laugh at first, but when we were leaving the restaurant he told me I had a good sense of humour. Marc and Ken lodged my steak knife into the cast on my hand so I could cut my own food for the first time.

When we left, I had to walk through a crowd of people by the door who were waiting for tables. They parted to let me through, some staring, others not knowing where to look.

"Don't sit too close to the grill," I said, as I passed them. I didn't look back. Marc pissed himself laughing.

If anything, people generally made me uncomfortable only by treating me too well. I could get away with just about anything. "No one hits the burn guy" is a saying I have developed over the years. I might never have realized that I was behaving badly if Marc hadn't put the kid gloves aside and been honest. I'd noticed his wife, Janice, was never around when I visited, and he told me she didn't want to see me because of some things I'd said to her, some jokes I'd made, which she found offensive.

"Why is she so sensitive?" I said. "I was just teasing."

"Yeah, I know you were, but she wasn't impressed," Marc said.

I was surprised by Marc's reprimand, but though I bristled at first, I knew he wouldn't say it if it weren't true.

One of my biggest problems had always been what I can only call controlling my mouth. Even when I was a kid, a comment would come into my head and before I had a chance to think about it, I'd said it. I can't even count the times my grandmother washed my mouth out with soap. I guess soap doesn't cure this condition.

During the rough patch before Tina and I split up, she told me some of her friends felt the same way Janice did. They didn't like being around me because of my tendency to make obnoxious remarks. I thought I was being funny, but I was actually hurting people, and that was hard to hear. I had always been a teaser, and people had often told me I was funny, but I began to realize that, since the fire, some of my "jokes" had become meaner. I think that meanness was one way I expressed the bitter feelings that had built up inside me. The only people I never teased were Tina—because I knew I couldn't get away with it—and, of course, Amber. I'd leave that to the kids at school; I wanted my daughter to always see me as someone safe, whose presence meant comfort and unconditional kindness.

The scriptures say, "A broken and contrite heart, oh God, you will not despise."

"So the most important attribute is humility," Pastor Habben told me. "A good Christian strives for a life pure in thought, word, and deed."

I'd always wished I had more humility. I knew it was a trait I sorely lacked. Admitting my mistakes and apologizing was one way I always tried to practise humility. But I still wish I were more humble. I wish I knew all the intricacies of it.

After some soul-searching, I told Janice, "I know I've lost your respect, and I have to earn it back. I was a bitter person, and I'm sorry." I said the same thing to Tina's friends whom I knew I'd offended.

I try hard now to think before I speak. I don't want to hurt anyone—I never did—but I have hurt people. It's a good sign that Janice and I get along well now, and she willingly spends time with me. I am always amazed at how forgiving people can be when we admit to our follies. Pastor Habben was wrong—humility isn't the most important attribute a person can have. I believe the most important attribute a person can have is forgiveness.

Forgiveness breeds humility, and that then breeds love. Love for life, love for others, love for oneself.

• • •

While I was still in intense daily rehab at the Millard Centre, I started volunteering at the Glenrose, at the prompting of David. He hadn't forgotten about our conversation the year before, when he suggested that I advocate for patients. He called me in to discuss program planning, and asked if I'd like to offer peer support for other patients with life-changing injuries. I went through formal training with Alberta Mental Health to speak with patients as a peer counsellor and started visiting burn and other patients. I listened and sympathized and told them how well my life was going, how I was finding self-acceptance and happiness.

David and I became quite close friends, and he even asked me for advice about carpentry and flooring for his home. One day, he approached me and asked if I'd speak at the Glenrose's upcoming fortieth anniversary gala about my accident and recovery. I'd spoken to him and many other people about my dream of speaking in public, so I wasn't going to say no to such an opportunity. Still, I was incredibly nervous. I spent hours and days writing the story of the fire and my rehabilitation, and practised reading it aloud. On the big night, I wore tear-away track pants, because I still wasn't good with buttons, and the white "Malibu" tee-shirt Dr. Montgomery had given me. When I stood up, all the chatting and laughing stopped. Everyone stared at me; there was dead silence. I read my fourteen-page presentation word for word, without looking up once. My hands shook the whole time, and I was sure I was speaking fast, in a completely monotone voice.

When I raised my head at the end of my talk, I saw a roomful of people with tears in their eyes. They started clapping; one person stood, and then another, and then the whole room. They gave me my first standing ovation.

I wasn't under any illusions about my speaking skills, but I went home that evening energized and excited. *I have a voice,* I thought. *I have something to say*. I started speaking in public more and more. Sharon and Diana, my physical therapist and occupational therapist from the U of A Hospital, both asked me to speak to their students. They said it would be a great asset for burn-care workers to hear about my experience of therapy. I talked to each class and answered their many questions.

I told those students a few things that made Sharon and Diana raise their eyebrows—like how I used to fake sleepiness to avoid therapy, and often even pretended to be asleep.

"That was news to me," Diana told me.

In my lecture to Sharon's class, I recounted one occasion when Sharon came in with the tilt table. It was important, Sharon tried to convince me, to get my body used to being upright; otherwise my heart wouldn't be used to pumping blood upward, and I'd get dizzy when I started standing and walking again. I hated the tilt table. I didn't think I'd ever get better, so I figured there was no point.

"So Sharon strapped me on," I told her students. "And as soon as she tilted me upright, I held my breath, inconspicuously. The oxygen level on my monitor dropped, so she lay me down again, and I started breathing, and my oxygen level went back to normal. After a few more times through this routine, Sharon called the respiratory specialist, who told her to forego therapy for the rest of the day. I went back to my room, and relaxed, watching TV."

When I finished telling the story, the whole class was laughing, and I didn't dare look at Sharon. After class, she just sighed and shook her head. She told me later how valuable it had been for her students to hear about that, to realize that depressed patients might resist their treatment in such sneaky ways.

Meanwhile, David sat me down again and said that Isabel Henderson, the senior operating officer at the Glenrose, had heard me speak at the fortieth anniversary gala, and wanted to meet with me. I'd stayed in the Glenrose for so long, but had never been in the main administrative offices before. David and I went together, and Isabel, an enthusiastic, friendly woman, welcomed me. She said she'd loved my presentation and wanted to help me reach more of the community. She told me about the annual National Rehabilitation

Nursing Conference, which would be hosted that year by the Glenrose, at the Fantasyland Hotel in Edmonton.

"The theme this year is Rehabilitation Nursing through the Ages," she explained, "and we're looking for a speaker to open the event on the first night. A keynote speaker. David has recommended you."

"You have so much insight into this," David added. "I really think the nurses would benefit from your story."

I rewrote my first presentation to focus more on my experience as a patient. I was still nervous, but more confident this time. To challenge my ability as a speaker I went without any notes. My parents were there, with Tina and her mother, at a table right in the front. That was the first time my parents heard the whole story of the fire, and they were among the first to start crying. Amazingly enough, in that roomful of experienced nurses, there wasn't a dry eye in the house. I was honoured to receive yet another standing ovation that night, and then spent the rest of the evening shaking people's hands and hearing congratulations. That's when I started to suspect it wasn't so crazy to think I could take my message further, to a wider audience.

And I had more than one message brewing. I wanted to tell people how I could have avoided the fire, about the macho attitudes that lead to so many accidents. I wanted to share how I'd freed myself from the anger and depression by accepting responsibility for what happened to me. I knew without a doubt that my optimism and inner strength depended on that revelation, and I rarely spent energy on anger toward the people I'd once blamed.

But I still had a major trial to face, quite literally. I was thrown for a loop in January 2006, when my former employer, Jack, was prosecuted under the *Occupational Health and Safety Act*, and I was asked to present a victim impact statement in court.

• • •

Trials

I begin each of my presentations by describing, play by play, my experience of the fire. Then I go on to talk about safety, overcoming depression and anger, or simply about being proud of who you are. I have different presentations for workers, executives, special-interest groups, health-care providers, and children. For each, I talk for forty-five minutes to an hour and a half, and when I finish speaking, I like to take questions.

Inevitably, the first guy to raise his hand (it's almost always a guy) wants to know, "What caused the fire?" I never explain that part as I recount the fire, because at the time, I didn't know.

The easy answer is that I was working with a volatile chemical in a new house. The furnace switched on, sucking air and highly combustive fumes into its belly. The furnace's engine sparked and ignited the fumes, which exploded, blowing the furnace apart, shooting back up the ducts and setting the liquid and vapours that surrounded me alight.

A more complex answer would include indirect but more significant causes, such as my complete lack of safety training and my willingness to follow orders without thinking for myself. It would include the machismo that let me feel invincible for the first twenty-nine years of my life, and which is so pervasive in the trades and in industry. That's why, at the beginning of each presentation, I always say I'm going to explain why I was hurt—not by listing the things my boss should have done differently, but by describing the things that I should have done. The things that I failed to do.

After I describe how the fire started, the audience members always want to know if I'm angry with my former employer—if he ever got his due. They want to know how I can live with what his negligence did to me. It's only human to want to hear that someone paid for what happened—that there was justice.

And they want to know why I seem so content. How I can be cheerful and confident, joking and smiling in front of hundreds of people, looking the way I do.

"Some people don't want to leave the house because of a bad haircut," one oil executive commented.

I struggled with thirst for vengeance and with pride, but my life is a non-starter if I let those impulses overcome me. I had to change my perspective so I could escape those traps, and Jack's trial was my last big hurdle to doing so.

• • •

I dreaded the court date, mostly because Jack would be there. All charges against the supplier and against the home builder had been dropped, and though at one point the home builder's insurance company even threatened to sue me for the damage to their property, those charges had been dropped when the home builder intervened on my behalf and absorbed the cost. Only the charges against Jack went before a judge. Unfortunately, in the great scheme of things, punishing Jack couldn't fix the real problem of unsafe practices among tradespeople constructing new houses. It's home builders who have the power to implement safe practices across the board. And with the right incentives, just as in the oil and gas industries, change can happen.

When the time came, I sat in the witness box and avoided looking at my former employer. It was the first time I would recount my whole experience. Of course, I'd spoken about the fire and my recovery many times, and several times in public, but I'd always avoided the most personal, gruesome, and humiliating details. As I spoke, the Crown prosecutor sat with Tina and held her hand.

I'd done many presentations before, even presentations about the fire, but this was different. I didn't know how to start, so I started by admitting that. "When I was asked by OH&S and the Crown prosecutor for a victim impact statement, I really didn't know where to start or what to say. Short of my will to live and to be a happy, productive part of society," I said, "my life has completely changed."

I talked about everything I'd missed while I was in the hospital, about everything I'd had to relearn, and about the pain, loss of dignity, and loss of independence. I recounted the fire and the hospital, and the strain on Tina. I spoke about Amber, what she'd go through. She would miss out on so many things other children do with their fathers. I couldn't play ball with her out in the summer heat, or take her tobogganing or ice fishing in the cold of winter. Amber didn't understand yet that I was different, but she would, and does now. To my amazement, she acts completely fine about "daddy being burned." She is very inquisitive, asks many questions, but loves her daddy completely. She is six, now. I hope that childhood innocence lives on. But let's face it—children love to harass each other, and I knew that my burns would make her an easy target. Since I refused to hide in my house, she would have to learn to defend herself, and likely to defend me, too. She would dread introducing her friends to me because of my disfigured face. Those, I said, were hardships beyond what any child should have to endure.

I would never have otherwise said some of those things out loud, but it was the right time and place for it. I recounted as many details as I could in those pages, and when I finished reading, the room was silent. The judge personally thanked me, as he was obviously moved by my openness to share so much, and said it was one of the best impact statements he'd ever heard.

Jack pled guilty to one of the charges, so the other eight counts were dropped. He was fined five thousand dollars, and required to donate thirty-five thousand to the U of A Hospital's Firefighters' Burn Treatment Unit, and thirty-five thousand to the Alberta Cancer Society because 901 is a known carcinogen.

His pleading guilty and being sentenced made no difference to me. No money, no jail time, no revenge could give back what my family and I had lost. All I wanted was for people to learn from his mistake, and for him to learn from his own mistake, the way he taught me. I wanted him to become a better employer.

In some ways, I don't believe Jack learned from what he did, from what happened to me. It's hard to overcome the tendency, which I've found in every employer I've ever had, to *blame the worker*. That attitude has been passed down from generation to generation. Even I was trained to think that way. The way we approach safety needs a paradigm shift. Thankfully that shift has started, but I believe we're fifty years away from seeing its full effects. All I can do is pray, and spread my story to companies that care about their employees.

And I have forgiven Jack. I reminded myself of what I had learned from him, about admitting to our mistakes and forgiving ourselves and others. It is too bad that the one piece of advice he gave me, which helped me so much to recover, he never learned himself. He never admitted his use of 901 was misguided. He never admitted he was wrong, too.

• • •

After the trial, I looked up the Material Safety Data Sheet for Roberts 1901. The one Jack had been required by law to provide me with. It took me about two minutes to find it online. I read 901's prescribed uses: "For cleaning tools and spills of adhesive." Of course, we'd all known this chemical was used mostly as a cleaner, but now I realized its manufacturer would never advocate pouring the stuff over such a huge area and certainly would not condone removing a houseful of linoleum with it.

I kept reading: "Vapours may cause flash fire, ignite explosively, travel along ground to remote source and flash back." It was all there! It had been there all along. If I'd only taken the time to read this MSDS. My entire ordeal had been entirely, easily preventable.

It was like a sick joke. "Solvent gloves should be worn. Goggles should be worn. In cases of large spills in a confined area, do not venture without a self-contained breathing apparatus with full-face piece." Well, I had spilled—poured—four full containers of 901 in a confined area, and had ventured in, in shorts and a tee-shirt.

Finally, just to add insult to injury, I focused on a line in the middle of the page. "Liver damage may occur in survivors of massive exposure to vapours." Once again, I had to face how easy it would have been for me to find the information that I needed to avoid the absurdly dangerous situation I'd put myself in, the full repercussions of which I had yet to discover, and to get it done safely.

• • •

As I tell my audiences, an unexpected thing happened while I was getting better. As I went through rehab at the Glenrose and Millard Centre, I met hundreds, if not thousands, of other people who'd been hurt. Most of them had been hurt at work, since that's the system I was in. When people saw me trying so hard to get better, they wondered what this severely burned guy had that was worth fighting for. Dave told me that he'd had clients depressed and overwhelmed by wrist or hand injuries who saw me working the elliptical machine for all I was worth and stopped their self-pity in mid-sentence, forever.

One by one, people gathered the courage to come over and introduce themselves, and before I knew it, they were telling me how they had been injured. I heard their own stories about the day their lives changed, and never did I hear about an accident, or "incident" as safety professionals say, that resulted from some complicated series of events. Usually—always—it boiled down to something simple, something overlooked, a shortcut, not following an employer's safety system, or just plain rushing to get it done. As I listened to more and more stories, I realized that all our injuries and their accompanying stories were completely different; and yet, we all got hurt for the same reasons.

All of us—especially men—were part of a culture that told us we were invincible, a culture most of us bought into when we were children, as we witnessed our parents using rickety chairs as ladders, mowing their lawns in sandals, and exercising their inalienable human right to drive without a seatbelt. As a culture, we accept that *boys will be boys,* that being tough or macho and getting hurt is just part of a man's life. When my dad used to take me fishing, he carefully bundled me into my life jacket, only to fluff up his as a cushion as he cracked his first beer, and most people grow up to demonstrate that same message to the next generation: that safety is for kids. The injured workers I met, like me, were part of a culture that didn't bother with proper safety equipment, at work or at home.

And I thought about the anger I saw in so many of my new acquaintances. They were angry because of their injuries, but they never said: "This happened because I wasn't paying attention. This happened because I didn't know enough. This happened because I was too tough to take care of myself."

I told those people how I'd come to accept how culpable I was for what happened to me. My errors weren't as obvious as offences against labour laws, but they were undeniable. I had put money first; I had never questioned my boss. I'd done whatever it took to get the job done. For a long time, those behaviours worked for me. I made good money and worked my way up to second-in-command. I was so successful, I couldn't see my faults, and after the fire, I came to see myself as a victim. When I found my own faults and admitted to them, I became empowered.

And I thought a lot about the factors that landed so many of us in the rehab hospitals on the Workers' Compensation Board's dime. I thought about all the guys and women out there, making the same mistakes we had, every day. It was clear to me that the culture that caused all those injuries, and was still causing more, needed to change. I remembered how my co-workers and I used to doze through what few safety meetings we attended. From what I heard, it was the same deal in the oil and gas industry. Sure, bigger companies had better safety policies in place, but the workers were no more interested in hearing about them. There had to be a way to get people to listen. And more than ever, I suspected I was just the person to find it.

• • •

Finding My Voice

"You know what I'd really like to do, if I could do anything? I'd like to be a motivational speaker."

Darlene, my career counsellor at the Millard Centre, was sitting across the desk from me. I'd been working with her since I approached Catherine, my Workers' Compensation Board caseworker, about looking for work. I was restless, sitting at home way too much. All I did was go to therapy and go out for dinner occasionally with my family. My volunteer work was satisfying but sporadic, and I didn't really have a life. I needed to get out. I needed to find an income, too. My allowance from WCB was small compared to what Tina and I were used to, and if things kept going the way they were, we'd have to sell the house and downsize everything.

"Sure," said Catherine. "But Spencer, you can't go back to your old job. You'll have to be retrained. What can you do?"

"I don't know," I admitted.

"You need a career counsellor and I know just the person: Darlene."

Neither of them was crazy about my public-speaking idea. The Workers' Compensation Board didn't want the risks that came with being self-employed; if they were footing the bill, I needed to find a career that was more stable, something that guaranteed me an income. Darlene echoed Catherine when she said there wasn't a lot of money in my idea, and that I needed to pursue something more practical.

"The whole idea of becoming a speaker is kind of like aiming to be a famous singer or actor," she said. "It takes time. You need to build up a reputation. It's a process, and you need a back-up plan, some education, just in case."

We brainstormed on what else I could do, and throughout the next few weeks, I almost drove Darlene crazy. Each time I saw her, she assigned me tasks. She told me to look through websites and take notes on jobs that interested me. I wanted to be an occupational therapy or physical therapy assistant, but Darlene said I couldn't do those jobs because of my hands. I was interested in electronics, but again, that work required dexterity. Of course, I couldn't do service because of my appearance, and Darlene pointed out I needed a flexible schedule because of my ongoing surgeries. Every day, I came up with new ideas and phoned Darlene.

"I have other clients, you know!" she joked. "Can't you work any slower?"

Then I started searching job-bank websites. As I scrolled through job after job, I came upon an ad: "Safety Advisor wanted." I searched "safety jobs" and discovered a whole field I never knew existed. I narrowed my search to "workplace safety," where my passion lay, and was amazed by all the career options. I phoned Darlene and told her about my idea, and she agreed it was a good fit. The next time I saw her, we talked about the construction safety jobs and WHMIS jobs, and discussed the skills they required. We looked at the skills I already had, and what kind of training I'd need.

"There's no reason why you can't do this," Darlene said. "You'll have to go back to school part-time, because it's hard to know when you'll be scheduled for surgery," she went on. "And we'll have to test your academic aptitude."

My aptitude test took place over an afternoon. I sat in a small room with a man named John, and he showed me pictures to test my perception. We went through math, memory, reading, and writing tests, as well as a visual perception test to see patterns, find what was wrong or missing in pictures, and recreate designs.

At the end of the afternoon, I watched him tally my scores. I was in the ninety-ninth percentile for visual perception, and my math was better than grade twelve, which was when I'd stopped studying it. I got 100 percent of the memory questions correct. I aced everything except reading and spelling, and he said I had the aptitude for a university education.

I stepped out of that room bellowing, "I'm a genius!"

• • •

I applied to the Alberta Construction Safety Association to get my safety professional certificate, and then I registered for the Occupational Health and Safety certificate program at the University of Alberta, Faculty of Extension. The first was bare bones; we learned about the Workers' Compensation Board forms and policies, and I finally took a WHMIS course and became a WHMIS instructor. I took the U of A course, too, because it was more in depth. I learned why the safety system is in place, how it's meant to work, and how it's implemented. And I experienced a university education, something I believed for so long wasn't in the cards for me.

My first day at university felt like the first day of grade one. I was nervous and self-conscious and had no idea what to expect. Then they changed rooms at the last minute, so I had to move. Since mobility was still a problem for me, it was a stressful first day. But I loved being back in school. In high school, I'd done the bare minimum, racing through my homework between classes and never doing any work outside school hours. This time was different. I actually read those textbooks front to back, took notes, studied my notes, listened in class, and participated. I learned a lot, and I learned I wasn't as smart as I thought I was. I still had so far to go. I saw how my teachers presented material, and I realized that while I could get my point across, I could be so much more engaging and powerful when I spoke. I was still thinking about the speaking career I really wanted, and saw school partly as a networking opportunity, to find new places to speak. It didn't hurt my confidence that I won the Glenrose's first Award of Courage and gave a short speech about courage when I was announced as the winner.

• • •

I applied myself to learning as much as I could about running a business as well as speaking. I knew the volunteer treasurer at my church had been doing the job for twenty-five years and wanted to pass on the position. What better way to learn to manage finances? I put the word out that I was willing, and before I knew it, I was in there, hook, line, and sinker. That position taught me how to balance books, do payroll taxes, and otherwise manage the finances for a business. I tell the congregants I'm on a five-year plan, but they say there's only one way out—I'm dying with their accounting books in my hands.

Another experience that showed me the value of clear expression occurred around Thanksgiving in 2005, when Grandpa Beach died of cancer. We began our turkey dinner that year by giving thanks for Grandpa Beach and all our memories of him, and after eating we talked until late, recounting our favourite stories of him. My family elected me to give a eulogy on behalf of my brothers and me, and I realized there was no way I could recount all those memories in my eulogy, no way I could choose the best out of so many meaningful moments. So I picked the theme: "If a picture is worth a thousand words then a memory must be worth a million."

The next day, I told the funeral guests my brothers and I each had a different relationship with our grandfather, and I summed up each in one word. For Reagan, it was *knowledge*; for Craig, it was *fishing*; for me, it was *friendship*. I talked about my apprenticeship at Beach Brothers, and how my Grandpa Beach had helped form the man I'd become. I talked about how he'd been there for me: visiting me in the Glenrose whenever he could and always comforting me with his presence.

When we left, the funeral director told me I'd given the best eulogy he'd ever heard. I was so grateful I'd honed the skills to write and deliver a speech worthy of Grandpa Beach and my affection for him.

• • •

David and Isabel continued to help me make contacts and were both convinced that speaking was my calling. My cousin helped me design my website, and Reagan helped come up with the name *Spencer Speaks*, my logo, and the brochure design. The vast majority of the wording and flow of the website and brochures is where my influence shows. Darlene didn't give up on my dream, either. She arranged for a Millard staff member called Robin, who belonged to the public-speaking club Toastmasters, to take me to a meeting.

I was hooked on Toastmasters immediately, although I felt like a fish out of water at my first meeting. I didn't think I was what they were used to at Toastmasters meetings. Fortunately for me, the public-speaking club was full of welcoming, friendly people who were serious about developing their skills and generous with their knowledge. It started to sink in that people could treat me well and accept me for who I am. Toastmasters is where I learned how to create a presentation, memorize it, and emote it. I learned to practise every hand movement and when to speak loudly or quietly, or just pause. When my club needed a VP of Education, they asked me, and I accepted the position. I eventually became president of the club.

Darlene introduced me to two more people who became invaluable mentors. The first was Fahreen, an employment specialist at the Millard. She ran a group called Steps, for injured workers training for new careers but having problems incorporating their injuries into their life. They were angry people, to say it simply, so my first regular speaking engagements were in front of a very hostile group. Fahreen was a quick-witted woman around my age who generously took me under her wing. She said I could speak to each of her groups, and that she'd give me feedback on my presentations.

The first time I spoke to Steps, I was so nervous that I couldn't sit down for hours beforehand. Darlene came to the talk, and I had to ask her afterward how I did, because it was all a blur. I was calmer the next time and realized what a great opportunity I had to hone my speaking skills and simultaneously motivate people who were depressed about abandoning their life's work after a newly acquired disability. After each talk, Fahreen and I strolled together down the long hallway back to the stairs, and she advised me on my text and delivery, on what was working and what still needed improvement. We came to call this routine the "long walk." I will always be grateful for Fahreen's kindness and compassion.

The other mentor I met through Darlene was Linda Schulze, who taught the computer class I was obliged to take before returning to school. The class itself was a breeze. I already knew most of what she was teaching and spent most of my work time sitting in the back corner, watching the other students struggle through what I'd finished in ten minutes. I think I made Linda a little nuts, too, calling her over and asking what I should do next. She told me later how amazed she'd been by my performance.

She also told me we were already connected. She'd heard about my accident on the news, on the night of April 24, 2003. The following Sunday, at her hometown church in Leduc, the pastor said, "You may have heard about the young man who was injured in the house explosion." He explained that my aunt Marilyn was part of the congregation, and she happened to be a close friend of Linda's.

"I couldn't believe it when Darlene asked me to include you in my class, and I realized you were that same Spencer Beach," she told me. "All this time I'd been praying for you, and here was my chance to help you."

She was apprehensive about teaching me because my injuries were so extensive, and I didn't help ease her anxiety when I showed up for the first class late, still dependent on home-care nurses and taxies that never showed up on time.

"I'll never forget when you knocked on the door, half an hour into class," Linda told me. "I pasted on my best professional smile, opened the door, and found myself staring squarely into your chest. I had no idea you'd be so tall. And why did you wear all black? Black ball cap, black glasses, black shirt, black polar fleece, dark jeans. You were impossibly thin back then."

It's a perfect example of my appearance's impact on other people, because I have no recollection of what I was wearing that day or even of interrupting the class, but that first glimpse of me will never leave Linda. She says it was like a "post-modern encounter with the ghost of Christmas-yet-to-come." You can tell she used to be an English teacher.

When I found out that was Linda's background, I told her, "I could use you!"

I asked her if she'd be interested in working for me as an editor, and she was excited about the prospect.

With Linda's help, I fine-tuned my process. First came the inspiration, and then I wrote out my presentation and read it aloud a couple of times. Finally, I tried performing it without notes, to see how it flowed. When I had a draft I was happy with, I sent it to Linda, and after a few weeks we met for coffee, where we argued and debated and hammered at that draft until I could work with it.

Hiring Linda as my editor was the best thing I ever did for my company. She took a good presentation and helped to make it great; she added nuances and jokes, and taught me to imagine how the audience would hear my words. She taught me the difference between "showing" and "telling," and encouraged me to insert dialogue and scenes in my story so it would come alive. We practised the entire performance, including when to pause and when to move, though she said those things came naturally to me. My weaknesses were in the writing, she said, but my great strength lay in the delivery.

After meeting with Linda, I always went home and practised. I memorized the introduction, the conclusion, all the key points, and the transitions. I didn't commit every word and phrase to memory, but I practised until I knew I could miss a line and pick up at any point. I practised in front of the mirror and in front of anyone who'd listen. Tina always felt strange about my presentations, so I stopped making her listen to them. She supported my goals and was proud of me for pursuing them, but the way I told my story disturbed her. There were things she remembered differently, just small details sometimes. Something I've noticed more than ever since the fire is that people remember things differently. And Tina was always such a reserved person; she didn't understand why I wanted to expose my story—and hers—in public. I was grateful to her for trying to understand why I had to do this. I didn't want to just have a job. I wanted to make a difference.

Linda was a dedicated teacher. She attended several of my talks and then described exactly how I was improving, how I was learning to work a room, and how my signs of nervousness were falling away. Before my first paid conference, Linda invited me to practise at her home, in front of her and her husband, who'd never heard or read my presentation before. When I finished, they were both in tears. They clapped, and Linda hugged me. She and her husband were moving away, so she wouldn't be my editor for much longer. She told me working together had been one of the most rewarding experiences of her life. And the event went as well as she said it would; in fact, when I received my cheque I realized they'd doubled my invoice!

• • •

During the first year I ran Spencer Speaks, Inc., I underwent physical assessments with a series of specialists. They assessed my lung capacity, nerve damage, joints, and movement. My whole body was assessed, inside and out. When the final tally came back, it revealed that I was over 100 percent permanently impaired. Now, that doesn't mean I'm useless as a rock; it doesn't mean I'm completely disabled; but it means that every function I perform is impaired in some way. Workers' Compensation Board legislation assumes if you hit 100 percent, there's no way you'll ever be able to do anything that would help society or generate an income. They guaranteed my income unconditionally until I was sixty-five.

I want to emphasize that I'm glad my Workers' Compensation Board income expires when I'm sixty-five, and that it was never enough to support my family. I never felt that my life should be handed to me on a silver platter. Many people injured at work don't have my options, and I know of families that struggle to make ends meet on government disability programs. My heart goes out to those people, and I believe that, as a society, we can and must do much more. For me, though, I think the worst thing would have been to receive millions of dollars. What would I have done with it? I probably would've blown it, and I'd still be in the boat I'm in now. It wouldn't have made Tina and me happy; it wouldn't have given me courage and strength. And without the need to support myself, I don't know if I'd have found the ambition to do everything I have.

I didn't look back. I had three speaking engagements in 2005, one paid. By 2008, I'd written six different presentations, and that year I spoke one hundred times. I loved every day of it. My goal was always to change one person in the audience, and I believed that I always achieved that goal. I never left disappointed. Since I'd worked in the trades for so long, I often saw people I knew in my audiences. Everyone had heard what had happened to me, so they weren't shocked by how I looked or where I'd ended up. They got their buffer period over with while I was talking, and then came to shake my hand or hug me. Following an event, I was always sure to get an email from an audience member telling me how I had affected his or her life. I was making that difference.

• • •

During that time, I started going to the gym again, because I wanted to play sports with my daughter and my nephews. I also hoped to slow down my metabolism so that my heart could handle heat better. Maybe then I could go out when it was hot, rather than sitting cooped up by the air conditioner. And of course I worked out because I wanted to feel good about myself; I may have had bumpy, patchwork skin, but at least I could have muscles. The only thing that I regret is how Tina and I fell into roles again—me as provider and she as mother and caregiver. I was so focused on rebuilding my ability to provide that I lost sight of my true roles as companion and nurturer, as engaged husband and father.

With daily therapy at the Millard my health and physical abilities were improving constantly, though each surgery temporarily set me back a bit. I was always pushing myself to make my life better. I learned how to skate again by pushing a lawn chair on the ice ahead of me. I looked like an idiot, but I did it. In 2008, I hired my fourteen-year-old nephew to help me build a patio behind my house. I wanted Tyler there to help just in case I needed it, and I was also happy to pass on some of my trades knowledge to him, as he'd always been interested in tools and building. Together, we finished that patio.

Some of my worst fears were somewhat founded. Some of my friends never accepted me. I still haven't seen my childhood best friend since the fire—he's seen the pictures and he can't deal with it. That's how people cope, sometimes, and I know that people who knew me best had the most challenging time accepting the changes. But my life was still full of people who loved me, and by getting over the fire and continuing with my life, I helped my family get over it, too. My parents and brothers, and my close friends, could go about their lives without the constant ache of having a damaged loved one. They had a burn survivor in their lives, but it wasn't the end of the world.

The only person in my life who still hadn't dealt with the fire was Amber. She hadn't noticed yet that anything was wrong with me. Occasionally she asked questions, like why my skin was patchy, and I told her, "Because I was in a fire." She accepted the explanation and went back to hugging me or playing. I knew eventually she'd realize there was more to my story, and she did. She realized more all the time, and started asking questions such as "What was it like to be in an ambulance, Daddy? Why do you need to go for this surgery, Daddy? I'll bring you a present. What happened to your fingers, Daddy?" I answered her questions truthfully. Amber is now in grade one. She's popular and happy, and her friends accept me easily. I have to admit that my fears about the effects of my burns on her life were completely misguided, at least so far. But then I have done everything possible to give her a loving, active, and honest father. She often tells me I'm the funniest dad, ever. And, like her dad, she can't tell a lie.

• • •

At one Toastmasters meeting in 2008, we each spoke about our dreams. Many members talked about money and travelling, and I understand wanting those things, but they seem to happen easily, with a little dedication. Those are goals, not dreams. We tend to make life so complicated. At that Toastmasters meeting, I first told them my childhood dream was to have wings and fly, but my dreams are simple now.

After I was released from the Glenrose, I started wondering how the fire, my exposure to 901, and my recovery had affected my life expectancy. I asked Dr. P. straight out, and he said, "You're probably not going to live to be eighty or ninety." I'll be happy if I make it to sixty. I may face liver disease or I could get cancer from my exposure to the chemical. My grafted skin is prone to cancer, and I still get deep infections that tunnel through my skin and into my tissue, and it takes months of antibiotics to cure them. My immune system has been weakened; I get colds and flus more frequently than the average person does.

So I just dream of a long life full of friends, family, and happiness. Strong mind, strong spirit, strong body, strong relationships. That's my dream and my key to happiness.

The Apples She Ate

In 2008, I discovered that the fire still had one more thing to destroy. That year, my marriage broke down, and I can say without hesitation it was the worst time of my life. Perhaps it speaks to the crux of the problem that I was perfectly content until one night Tina tapped me on the shoulder in bed as I said my silent nighttime prayers. I finished praying before I turned to her.

"What's up?" I asked.

"I'm not happy," she told me. "I haven't been happy for a long time." She told me she was thinking of divorcing me.

I shouldn't have been shocked; after all, I had heard this story countless times in rehab from other injured people, and I knew the divorce rates for burn survivors were much higher even than for those with severe injuries in general. But I was shocked. I had convinced myself that Tina and I would always be together, that we would beat all the odds. I'd thought we were doing well, that we were happy, a success story, after everything we'd been through. Over the following weeks, I panicked, analyzed, and reasoned. I couldn't sleep; I stayed awake day after day. I lost interest in my work and in the volunteer positions I held. I became sad, bitter, and angry. I felt destroyed.

I thought about Dr. Prichard, how whenever I'd seen him since I came home, his first question was, "How's Tina?"

He knew what she'd been through, and it's rare that anyone truly understands what Tina endured after the fire. In a situation as dire as mine, the spouse always has it worse that the person injured. I believe the stress I suffered was minute compared to Tina's. While I was lying in bed, unconscious or semi-conscious, Tina was alone and pregnant, running the household, taking care of the bills and other banking, and dealing with the media and the doctors. Every night, she wondered if I'd still be alive in the morning; every day, Dr. P. told her which of my fingers he'd amputated and which of my organs was failing. As she became a single parent, the long-term future was a complete uncertainty.

When I finally moved back home, Tina effectively had two babies to care for. While I fought to survive and get my basic functions back, she fought for everything else and worried about the rest. Dr. P. knew no one was as strong as my wife seemed. He knew all the stress and unexpressed emotions were building up inside her. Add all that to the pre-existing tensions in our marriage, the basic conflicts that arose from my extreme extroversion and her reserved ways, and it's not hard to understand what went wrong. Five years after my accident, I was completely independent, and at the same time, our daughter began kindergarten. Tina had been living for me and Amber for five years, and now she had time on her hands: her own time, and lots of it. The trauma of the previous five years, and the fact that she'd lost sight of her own goals, hit her like a landslide.

My speaking career was hard on Tina, too, because she couldn't understand why the whole world needed to hear our story. When I told Dr. P. I was writing a book, he was hesitant, because he was afraid the publicity would hurt her.

"Tina's a wholesome, decent person," he said. "And a private one. Are you sure this is what she wants?"

Tina and I decided together to go ahead with the book, and I gave her the option to stop it. She didn't want to stand in my path, but I know this was hard on her, too.

• • •

In 2009, I entered the annual Toastmasters competition and came in second for the area competition with my talk about living for the moment. I told my audience about my separation from Tina; I told them I'd lost more than a wife. I lost my best friend and the best person I'd ever known.

Then I said, "All is not lost; I have recently found myself, and thus happiness, again. In a way, I owe my wife a huge thank you for her words and actions. She showed me I was living in a routine, and not living in a life."

Despite everything I'd learned from the fire, I'd caught myself in the old trap of living for tomorrow. I realized that everything I'd been doing, from volunteering, planning, and dreaming, to my family life, was all about securing the future. I took my wife for granted, my daughter's time wasn't as precious as it should have been, and I'd even started putting off my own interests, like skiing, golfing, camping, and hanging out with friends.

I realized when my marriage ended, just as economic recession decreased my speaking engagements, that my future was completely uncertain. And it still is—it always was, and it always will be. All I know is, my future is controlled by one entity, and that's God. Not only does He know what the future holds for me, He's created that future. I think Pastor Habben explained it best when he said we have choices, but God already knows the choices we're going to make. So, just choose one.

I urged that Toastmasters audience to take advantage of the joy today brings. Of course it's important to plan, but far too many people go around today trying to complete what they planned yesterday and crowding tomorrow with more plans still. When they get a day off, they have no idea what to do. They've forgotten how to live for today. When I came to see the error of my ways, I found a new lease on life. I live each day to its fullest. Of course, my shift in attitude wouldn't have been enough to save my relationship with Tina. Our relationship and its fallout taught me more than I can possibly recount here, and nor should I recount such private matters. When Tina left me, it hurt me more than going through the fire. She is my first love and my one true love. Although I was hurt by her, I tried to focus on why she wanted a divorce, rather than on the pain of losing her. I put myself in her shoes, and was able to imagine behaving the same way. I found my eyes were opened to the truth instead of closed by the anger.

I've learned so much about love. Back in the early days of my volunteer work at the Glenrose, I met a teenaged burn patient I'll call Josh. He wasn't as extensively burned as I was, but he had worse facial scarring and was severely depressed. His words sounded all too familiar as he described his fears about maintaining friendships, doing meaningful work, and finding love. His girlfriend from before the injury hadn't stuck around.

He asked me, "Do you think I'll ever find love again?"

"Listen," I said. "If I wasn't married right now, I think I'd have a girlfriend. I'd have my pick. You'll find love," I assured him. "Women see the beauty in people."

A few years later, Josh came to one of my engagements, and he introduced me to the pretty, charming girl at his side as his girlfriend. It felt great to have helped that young man find the confidence he needed. And I looked back on that experience when Tina and I separated. Once I was living alone, I found my old attention-seeking, flirtatious self re-emerging, but the notion of dating was daunting. All those old thoughts came rushing back—*Why would anyone choose this*?

One thing I knew for sure was that I didn't want to go back to the way I was before the fire, or before I met Tina. I remembered the unwholesome relationships I'd let into my life, both with friends and lovers. I'd go out and hit on a girl just to hit on someone, just to play the game, and then I was perplexed when, instead of finding a relationship with depth, I found myself in yet another sexual drama that fizzled out within a month or less. When I did find the right person, it was wonderful, but I clung on too hard and too quickly, and never had a chance to get to know Tina as a friend before getting seriously involved. My advice for Amber when she gets older will be: don't go looking for love. Instead, go and live your life, be happy with who you are, and let love find you.

• • •

On our tenth anniversary, I wrote Tina a note saying, "I don't know why I love you; I just do. And that's the way it should be." I told her love should not be simple enough to sum up in words; there were things I loved about Tina, including her flaws, and new things I discovered every day. Love, I said, should be given openly, embracing the whole person. But when she told me our marriage wasn't making her happy anymore, I realized there were hundreds of specific things I loved about her. I wrote a list. I remembered how she sat beside my hospital bed, pregnant and no doubt exhausted, reading to me from her notebook. When she ran out of news and conversations to report, she described how she chose between a red apple and a green apple in the grocery store.

Tina saw things in that hospital that no one should ever see. Sometimes when she came into my room, she couldn't believe the state I was in; the worst was the first time she saw me, with no warning, without bandages and missing most of my skin. It was terrible for both of us. Not only had Tina seen things that traumatized her, it was *me* she'd seen. And after all that, she was still the only person who could see through my burns. To her, I was just Spencer. As years passed, many people brought up the burns constantly, either in a question or in a joke. They simply couldn't get over the scars. I got over them and the way I look largely because Tina did. She still loved me and it didn't matter what the rest of the world thought.

Though our lives are separate now, I'll always remember how Tina stood by me, sometimes hauling me back up from the depths of depression and delusion, often giving me comfort simply by sitting at my side. What we went through together brought us close in a way most people never experience, and because of Tina sticking with me, there's a little girl now who has a dad.

As of today, Tina and I live separately, but she is still my best friend. We have cancelled the divorce, and together we are slowly working through the messes we have made. I have hope that one day we will be a family again. The Bible reminds us that a husband should love his wife as Christ loved the church. What an awesome example to follow. I will walk now beside Tina, supporting, praying, waiting, loving, and accepting—unconditionally. I know she loves me, and I her, and that sometimes in life it hurts to love someone. I am sorry for putting Tina through the fire. If there is any regret that I will die with, it will be how the fire affected her.

When I wrote my list for Tina, I told her, “I love you because you told me about the apples you ate.” What I meant was, *without you, I wouldn't have survived.*

• • •

Acknowledgements

First, I thank God for giving me more days to enjoy, full of people I love. I am grateful to everyone at the University of Alberta's Walter C. Mackenzie Health Sciences Centre who worked so hard and cared so much for me and my family, including all the support staff who worked behind the scenes, especially Blanche. Thank you to all my moms and dads and brothers and sisters, who love me no matter what skin I wear, and who were there for Tina and me when we needed you the most. Val, Sharon, Maria, Dave, Linda, Kaysry, Penny, Caitlin, Darcy, Deb, Dave, Jim, and Diana—you were with me through so much pain, and you got me back home. Linda, Darlene, Isabel, Mary, and Fahreen, you helped me achieve my dreams. Dr. Mann, you saw my darkest demons and taught me I am not crazy. May your river always flow smoothly! To all the staff at the Glenrose Rehabillitation Hospital and Millard Health Centre: you have my deepest gratitude. All my home-care nurses took away some of Tina's burden when I first came home; I think they saw me fight the hardest. I thank my true friends for always challenging me to never give in, and my new friend Naomi; you never know when fate will have two people meet. And my church family—God sure does know what is best for me, and people like you are what He had in mind. Thank you so much for everything. It truly has been an adventure.

—Spencer Beach

I am grateful to Lyn Cadence, Charlene Dobmeier, Lauren Krugel, Nomi Claire Lazar, David Lewis, Jason Markusoff, Mar'ce Merrell, Shannon Montgomery, Bill Novak, and the members of Calgary's Kensington Writers Group for invaluable help and advice. For time, expertise, and candour, I thank the many people interviewed for this project, especially the Beach family, Pastor Dan Habben and the staff of the University of Alberta Firefighters' Burn Treatment Unit, the Glenrose Rehabilitation Hospital, and the Millard Health Centre. Kimberley and Henry Howard generously offered me their home and hospitality in Edmonton. And Spencer Beach humbled me with his trust and with his breathtaking honesty.

—Naomi K. Lewis

About the Authors

Spencer Beach is a professional speaker and workplace safety advocate. He was a floor layer for many years, graduated from the University of Alberta's Occupational Health and Safety program, and is a certified Construction Safety Professional. He grew up in St. Albert, Alberta, and lives in Edmonton. His website is www.spencerspeaks.ca.

Naomi K. Lewis is a writer, editor, and teacher in Calgary. Her website is www.naomiklewis.com.